Whispers From God

Whispers From God

The Kaleb Davis Story

Laneice Davis

Copyright © 2009 by Laneice Davis.

ISBN: Hardcover   978-1-4415-7793-1
          Softcover   978-1-4415-7792-4

All rights reserved. No part of this book may be reproduced or transmitted in any form or by any means, electronic or mechanical, including photocopying, recording, or by any information storage and retrieval system, without permission in writing from the copyright owner.

Cover and author picture by: Cindy Powers-Moser

All medical names have been changed to protect their privacy

This book was printed in the United States of America.

To order additional copies of this book, contact:
Xlibris Corporation
1-888-795-4274
www.Xlibris.com
Orders@Xlibris.com
61345

Contents

Preface 9

Chapter 1   Windstorm 11

Chapter 2   Entering the Valley 16

Chapter 3   Strength from Above 23

Chapter 4   The Valley of the Shadow of Death 29

Chapter 5   Touched by an Angel 37

Chapter 6   New Friends . . . New Places 44

Chapter 7   There's No Place Like Home 50

Chapter 8   Listening To God 56

Chapter 9   Another Valley, Another Victory 63

Chapter 10   Our God is Awesome 68

Many Thanks 71

Epilogue 73

Dedication

This book is first and foremost dedicated to God. Without Him, I'm convinced this would be a short book with a very sad ending. It is by His grace that we are where we are today. I give Him all the glory. May He add His blessings to this book.

Next, this book is dedicated to my entire family. Without their help we would have never been able to get through this valley.

Finally, it is dedicated to the people of Ashe County. Their support has been matchless. No words could ever express our gratitude.

PREFACE

As I sit and try to concentrate on writing this book, I am constantly interrupted and lose my train of thought. It is the distraction of giggles from my living room, cartoons playing on the TV, and children chasing dogs through my freshly cleaned house. It is the sound of everything I just picked up, being pulled back out to be looked at for about 30 seconds, and then left for me to pick up again. It is also the sight of dirty dishes laying on the counter that I know will not wash themselves. But more than anything, it is the thought of THANK GOD there are giggles in my living room, cartoons playing on my TV, and two wonderful, healthy children to enjoy the things we are blessed with.

You see, before Kaleb's accident, I used to get so upset with my children for running through the house. Let's face it, I think every parent in the world, at one time or another, has said, "If I tell you one more time to stop running in this house . . . ." One day right after we got home from the hospital, I was outside working in my flower garden. My work was interrupted by the sound of wild feet running through the house, a freshly cleaned house I might add. I stood up and was on the verge of shouting, "Kaleb Davis, I have told you about running in the house!" Then I stopped myself for that could not be Kaleb. It was footsteps I heard, not the sound of a wheelchair rolling across the floor. So I walked quietly up my front porch steps and peeped in the window.

I saw Mollie, my very active daughter, running full blast all over the living room and bouncing on the couch cushions. I also saw Kaleb, my very injured son, sitting in his wheelchair loving every minute of watching her. He was shouting out commands and dares for Mollie to try next. My blood ran cold. I took just a moment to look at this new 'normal' scene that we were left with after the accident. I opened the door and immediately saw the 'deer in the headlights' look from my children. I said, "If we are going to do this, let's do it right." I grabbed hold of Kaleb's wheelchair, popped the biggest wheelie I could, and chased Mollie all over the house. We laughed, we played, we turned the music up loud, and we danced.

We were always a close family. I know that, with God's help, that will never change. What changed, however, was my attitude about what mattered most. Growing up in rural Ashe County, North Carolina, I learned early on that family and community is a big part of who you are. The people who live in Ashe are a very tight knit group. The people are quite different than those you might meet elsewhere.

If someone is in need, it is a certainty that the need will be filled far beyond what one could ever fathom. I learned this during the four months of Kaleb's hospital stay. Everyone offered us gifts beyond what we ever imagined. However, the greatest of all the gifts we received were the prayers of God's people.

My hope for you, as you read this book, is that you understand that nothing, not even life itself, is more important than our relationship with our Heavenly Father. He has given us so many joys here on this earth, and I feel we do ourselves a great injustice by not taking full advantage of them. Yes, we have children, we have family, we have material possessions; these are all wonderful things that we should not take for granted. But more importantly, we should not take for granted the promise of eternal life. It is my prayer that if you don't already have this promise, you will talk to someone who does. Talk to a preacher, talk to a friend, talk to a mother or father, but more than that—talk to God. You never know when you will really need Him.

CHAPTER 1

Windstorm

"Kaleb, get ready, we're late!"
"Mollie, I don't know why in the world you want to do that."
"No, Kaleb, not now, I'm busy."
"Mollie, please be still, I don't have time right now."

These sentences and many more ran through my mind countless times, as I sat beside my child and tried to pray that he would just live. What would it have hurt to put those bunk beds up in his room? Sure they took up a lot of space, but it was his space and he wanted them. Why did we ditch out that soggy bottom beside our house and just leave it, when there was enough water there to make the fish pond he wanted so badly? I sat and took a good long look at my life and asked what was so important that I couldn't just relax, enjoy my children, and love the Lord the way we are commanded to do. Then usually an alarm would sound, and the doctors and nurses would run in. My thoughts would once again return to, "Please God, just let him live."

Let me take you back to an evening in September 2002. I was lying in bed doing my usual prayer time, you know, "Thanks God for the day, help me be a better person, guide me and show me what you would have me do." Oh, how I was stuck in a routine!!! I had tried to get out of this habit by starting a prayer journal. Every night I would pray to God and ask for a scripture for the evening, open my Bible, read the scripture, then write down in my journal what I thought the verse or verses meant to me at that time.

This night though it was different. I had opened my Bible to Zechariah 6:11-13,

> "Then take silver and gold, and make crowns, and set them upon the head of Joshua the son of Josedech the high priest: and speak unto him, saying, Thus speaketh the Lord of hosts, saying, Behold the man whose name is The BRANCH; and he shall grow up out of his place, and he shall build the temple of the Lord: Even he shall build the temple of the Lord; and he shall bear the glory, and shall sit and rule upon his throne; and he shall be a priest upon his throne: and the counsel of peace shall be between them both."

I actually wrote in my journal, "I'm not sure what I should get from this scripture. I know God is preparing me for something. I cannot tell yet what it is. I just know that I should have faith." I remember thinking about this verse and trying to apply it to my life at the time. I understood the "BRANCH" was Jesus, but what could this mean for my life now? After that, days passed, then months, but nothing else came to me. Other entries were made in my journal, but each time was the same thing, "God is preparing me for something."

Then on May 30, 2003, I began the journey God had been preparing me for. It was Memorial Day weekend. My family and some of our good friends had planned a camping trip. We were going to stay Friday, Saturday, and come home on Sunday. I had expressed a concern about the trip. I did not want to go. It seemed like a long time in a tent, and we would be missing church services. But after seeing the excitement on my children's faces and knowing what it meant to them, I decided to go.

I had to work late that Friday, so everyone else went on without me, and I came by myself. When I arrived at the campground, the owner had to take me on a golf cart to our site, because a car could not get there. I still had a very uncomfortable feeling, but as usual did not listen to that 'still small voice.' What I did though, was walk around the campsite and ask God for His protection. I was very worried about this trip and could not find peace with it. However, Friday night was very uneventful and all things considered, we were having a very nice time.

On Saturday the rain came. It rained and rained, so we spent a lot of time inside the tents playing cards and just hanging out. Saturday evening the sky cleared off some, and the wind picked up. My sister and her family came to visit us. We grilled out and just sat around the fire talking. At one point Kaleb, who was 11 years old at the time, came over and just sat beside me. I remember asking him what was wrong. He said, "Nothing," but just looked sad. Even my sister made the comment that he was acting a little different. Kaleb told us later on that nothing was wrong. Actually, he said that he had had a very good feeling. He felt as though he was on top of the world and that nothing could stand in his way. God must have been preparing him. Then night started to fall, and our guests began to leave. We all said our goodbyes, and the wind began to blow harder.

Kaleb and my husband's brother, Brant, were playing horseshoes in the field beside our campsite. Tom, my husband, was walking around in the same area. My friend, Dreama, her daughter, Summer, her son, Daniel (who is Kaleb's age), Mollie, and I were all sitting around the campfire just enjoying the evening. I looked up in the sky and saw a very large tree limb falling. I told Dreama to look and we all just sat there and watched this limb fall from the sky. Little did I know how this one limb was about to change the life of my son, myself, and everyone around us.

The next thing I saw was Brant jumping, waving his arms, and screaming for help. Believe it or not, I still did not realize what had taken place. I remember turning to Dreama and saying, "Oh no! I bet that limb hit Brant's truck!" Then it happened. I will never, ever forget the next thing I heard. It was terror, nothing but terror from my husband screaming, "Kaleb, please, no! Don't do this to me. You can't die! Not now, please Kaleb!" It seemed like he just kept screaming and I could not get there. I was running but getting no where. All of a sudden, I was face to face with my son lying on the ground with a huge tree limb covering his small, lifeless body. He was not breathing, and his lips already seemed blue.

I ran as fast as I could back to the truck to call 911. I could not get the call to go through. I just kept dialing the number and crying; and all the while, I could hear Tom, my pillar of strength, falling to pieces. How could this be happening? Had all of those prayers I had been praying over the weekend been in vain? Or worse, was God not there for me? Had He even heard my prayers? Oh, how I needed Him right now—without delay. I was reminded of being a small child in my bedroom, in the middle of the night, screaming for my daddy. Where was he? I would lie there listening for his steps coming down the hall to hold me. Oh, how scared I was. Then my thoughts were once again interrupted. In the middle of all the screams of terror, running of friends, and that stupid busy signal in my ear, I heard it—a small whimper that could only be from my son. It's him, I hear him, and he needs his mom. I turned to see my husband cradling my child, and Kaleb was crying. He was really crying, so that meant he was alive. This is when I realized that the reason I didn't hear God's steps coming was because He was already there. He never leaves us, not even for a second.

Tom handed Kaleb to me in the truck and ran to the driver's side to leave for the hospital. We knew time was at hand and we had to act fast. Words could never describe the guilt that I feel for what happened next. My precious little girl, Mollie, who was seven years old at the time, was running to get to her brother and family. As I said time was of the utmost importance, so we just shut the door of the truck and yelled to Danny Farmer (Dreama's husband) to get Mollie. We just left that sweet little child with them. She no doubt was just as scared as we were, yet we left her. I knew she was in very good hands, but she needed her mommy as much as Kaleb did. Mollie and I have had a long talk about this since the accident, and I have done all I can to make this up to her. I just thank God that He has given me opportunities to make things right with Mollie.

In the truck on the way to the hospital, Kaleb started waking up more, and he began to speak to us. I finally got the call through to 911 and asked an ambulance to meet us on Highway 16. Kaleb looked up at me and asked, "What happened?" I explained that a tree limb had hit him, and we were on our way to the hospital. He asked me if he was going to die. I kept saying with all the strength, faith, and determination I could gain, "No, Kaleb, you are not going to die!" Then he turned to me and said, "We better pray." So we all began to pray, Kaleb leading the group. He just kept begging God not to let him die. Over and over again, this child pleaded desperately with God to let him live.

Then a long moment of silence filled the truck cab. I'm not sure how long it was or even what I was thinking at the time. I just know it was silent. This silence was soon overtaken by shouts of victory. Kaleb started shouting and praising God. "Oh, thank you God, I know I won't die! Thank you, thank you, thank you!" Then without any hesitation, or any fear of what others would say or think, he began to sing *Amazing Grace*. Never before or since have I ever heard anyone sing this song with so much heart and soul. Kaleb had a message from God Almighty Himself, and he was not ashamed to give God all the honor for it right then and there.

By this time, we had arrived at the appointed meeting place with the ambulance. Our truck and the ambulance pulled up at the exact same time. It had to have been planned by the Divine Spirit of God. We did not have to sit there and wait; the paramedics did not have to look for us; we just pulled up together. As I opened the truck door with Kaleb in my arms still praising God, Danny, Dreama, Daniel, Summer, Brant, my sister, Dawn, her husband, Dan, and of course Mollie came running up to the door. As I looked at all their faces the only thing I saw was fear, fear like I have never seen before in my life. All I could say was, "He is okay. He will be okay." What else could you say, when God had revealed to us in that old dirty truck cab, that yes, 'Daddy' heard your screams at the campsite and you did not hear His footsteps coming because He was already there!

With a pleading heart, I asked the paramedics if I could please ride with Kaleb to the hospital. Thank God, as they loaded my child, with a broken body but a grateful spirit, I climbed in right behind. We were on our way to Ashe Memorial Hospital for what would turn out to be a very, very long night.

Once we arrived at the hospital, our parents and my husband's other brother, Jeff, had all made it there in time to see Kaleb as he was whisked into the E.R. Tom and I went back with him and waited as Dr. Ryan Goodman carefully examined Kaleb. The main complaint we kept hearing was, "My arm is gone and my stomach hurts!" Of course x-rays were ordered, and Tom and I were asked to wait outside for Kaleb.

The waiting room was filled with family and friends. A lot of crying and praying was taking place. I am not real sure which we did the most—cry or pray. We are a very close family. I have only one sister, Dawn, who is seven years younger than me. The age difference made us close, because I helped to take care of her. She is married to Dan Powers, and they have three beautiful children. Silas is the oldest, followed by Bella, then finally little baby Asher. Dawn is a very good mother and a great sister. My parents, Bill and Linda Powers, have been married for 40 years. I feel like I have the best parents in the world. They have always supported me and I am frightened to think where I would be today without them. Growing up, I knew the two things I could always count on was my Heavenly Father and my family.

Tom is the middle son of Bob and Alene Davis. They have been married for 50 years, and like my family, they are very close. Jeff is the oldest, and Brant is the youngest. Brant was born when my husband was 13. So, like Dawn and me, Tom and Jeff helped to take care of Brant. Needless to say when Tom and I got married in 1987, our two families merged into one. It's hard to think of my life without Tom and his family being a part of it. We are truly blessed with family and friends. I could no doubt write an entire book about our loved ones. Maybe one day I will. We are so blessed to be part of such a great group of people.

Back in the waiting room minutes seemed like hours, but soon we were greeted by Dr. Sandra Thompson. She explained that Kaleb had a broken forearm, and she would like to set it with the help of another doctor whom she had paged. She felt like after the arm was set, and Kaleb had spent the night in the hospital, we could all go home in the morning. I was relieved to some extent, but the still small voice inside me said, "Prepare yourself, this is not over."

Tom and I were allowed to go back and stay with Kaleb as we waited for the doctor to return the page. Everyone else took turns coming back to be with us. We waited and waited. Dr. Thompson finally came in and said it was very unusual, but the doctor had not returned her call. She wanted to admit Kaleb and do the surgery in the morning. We agreed. Then Dr. Goodman entered the room and said, "I don't mean to alarm you, but I would just feel more comfortable if we sent Kaleb on, to another hospital that has neurologists and other specialists in case something else should go wrong. Would you mind if we sent him to Winston-Salem?" Without any hesitation, Tom and I both agreed to go to Baptist Hospital. Another ambulance was called, and we were told, unfortunately, we could not ride along this time.

Chapter 2

Entering the Valley

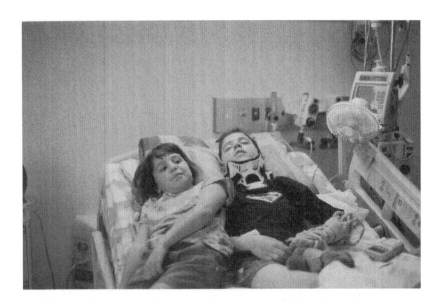

Kaleb was put in the ambulance, and after tearful goodbyes and exchanges of cell phone numbers, we left. The ambulance driver explained the route they would be taking, but advised us not to try to keep up; just drive safely down, and they would stay with Kaleb until we got there.

Tom, Mollie, and I climbed back into the truck and headed straight for Winston, with a caravan of family and friends behind us. The trip, although only an hour and a half, seemed to take much longer. Tom and I had made a deal not to call the ambulance cell phone until we were in Miller's Creek, about a half hour away. We called and found that Kaleb was sleeping and doing great. The paramedics told us that he had cooperated with everything they needed to do for him and was on his best behavior the entire trip.

We reached the emergency entrance to the hospital around 11:00 p.m. We were like 'fish out of water' at this very large and intimidating place. We pulled up to the main entrance to try to find a spot close to park, so we could just run in the hospital. There was no spot available. I jumped out of the truck and said to Tom, "You go park the truck somewhere, while I try to find Kaleb." I was one mom getting to her baby, and the lack of a parking space was not going to stop me! As I jumped out of the still moving truck, a security guard came up and asked if we needed help. I just kept going. He would just have to talk to my husband, I had somewhere to be at that moment. I ran through the hospital doors and was met by another officer. I said, "I'm looking for my son. He was brought here by an ambulance from Ashe County. Can you help me?" The officer said, "I know exactly where your son is! Let's go see him!" He took me straight into a room where my child laid sound asleep without a care in the world. You see, it's funny how innocent children only have to hear the Father's promise one time, then they rest assured that He does not lie! Kaleb was asleep and enjoying the word of the Lord that was spoken to him in our truck some three hours earlier.

I walked over to Kaleb and brushed his hair with my hand and softly spoke, "Mommy's here." He just smiled and said, "I'm sleepy." About that time in came Tom with a smile, and he said, "The first security guard we saw is going to park the truck for us, so I could follow you in to see Kaleb." Tom had also spoken to the paramedics who had been on the ambulance. They were amazed at how calm and relaxed Kaleb had been the entire trip. They told Tom that they had never brought a patient down that was so understanding and well behaved. Thank God for the peace He had spoken to my child. As we were talking, an older doctor walked in and introduced himself to us as Dr. Scott Jones. He explained that he would be Kaleb's main doctor and be in charge of seeing to his recovery. He also told us that the x-rays that were taken at the hospital in Ashe County had somehow been smeared. He was not able to see everything he wanted to on the x-rays, so he had taken more. He had also ordered a CAT scan. The only thing he knew, at this point, was that Kaleb did indeed have a broken arm, and he was afraid there were more injuries.

Kaleb was taken to the CAT scan with mom at his side. The images were taken, only to find that they still did not meet this fussy doctor's expectations. I cannot count how many scans were taken that night, but I can tell you it was more than a few. We just kept going to get the scans, then back to Kaleb's room, only to find they still were not what everyone was looking for; so back down we would go. This went on until around 12:00 a.m. Sunday morning. Finally all the tests were done, and we had a final word on his injuries. Kaleb's arm was not only broken, but he had a complete brachial plexus injury. The nerves that come from his spinal cord and feed his left arm were injured. There was too much blood to determine the extent of this injury. He also had a bruised liver, lacerated spleen, bruised lung, and a blood clot in his shoulder. The blood clot took top priority. Dr. Jones explained that Kaleb would be sent down to the operating room for a procedure using some type of balloon to remove the blood clot, but while we were waiting another doctor would come in and set his arm where it was broken. With the brachial plexus injury there would be no need for anesthesia, because he did not have any feeling in his arm anyway. I kept Kaleb's head turned towards me while the doctor took hold of his arm, lifted it up, and SNAP right into place it went! Kaleb lay on the table, looking at me, and didn't even flinch. Oh, how my arm ached just watching. And, oh, how thankful I was to God that Kaleb did not feel a thing.

By now it was around 6:30 a.m. on Sunday, June 1. Kaleb was taken to the operating room for the doctor to remove the blood clot from his shoulder. We were so exhausted. Our family was still in the emergency room waiting room. We had been taken down back hallways with Kaleb, so we didn't know how to get to them to let them know where we were. A member of the hospital staff took us to another waiting room to sit and wait for the surgery to be performed. Tom and I sat alone in the dark, lonely waiting room. Kaleb had been taken away, and we were left alone to wait, and wait, and wait. Oh, how helpless I felt. I could not think anymore. I could not feel my body. Nothing was normal. Everything looked different. Exhaustion had set in, and I did not know if I could go any farther. I found a restroom and went inside. It was dark and quiet. No one was there except me. I thought maybe this had been a dream, or had the end of time come and I was sentenced to this 'hell on earth?' Why was I here in the bathroom at a hospital and not getting ready for church? That's when I remembered we were going to have a Bible study this morning. What was there to stop me from fulfilling this plan? Now, of all times, I needed a Bible study. So I went back out to the waiting area and sat down beside my husband and quietly had a Bible study with God.

It was nearing 7:00 a.m., and the staff were starting to enter the hospital. I remember watching them come and go. They were all talking, laughing, and making plans for their day. I couldn't stop myself from thinking, "How can you just go on? Don't you know my son is in surgery? He is just a baby, and if that blood clot moves he could die." I must have dozed off with my thoughts, when all of a sudden, I woke up to see one of the orderlies who had wheeled Kaleb down to surgery. He was smiling and said, "I was just inside and Kaleb is doing great. Try not to worry, they are doing everything they can to help him." It was just enough hope to carry me through the rest of the wait. I stepped outside to use my cell phone to call home. I called Cathy Finley, who was my boss at the time. I explained what had happened and asked if she would please have her church pray for Kaleb. This was the first of many such requests that I would make over the next few months. When I returned to the waiting room, I found my husband sitting in the chair alone praying. You see, God was our only hope.

The doctor came out and said the clot could not be removed, so Kaleb would be sent upstairs to the Pediatric Intensive Care Unit (PICU). It would take a while to set things up and get him settled. They would let us know more when they could. By this time our family had found us and come into the waiting room. We filled them in on what was going on, and we all just sat and waited. Again our hearts were filled with prayers. Sometimes I wonder what God thought at this time. Did He get annoyed with us? Were we asking too much? Were we getting on His nerves? I don't think so. I think God was sitting in that waiting room with us. Yes, He was waiting to reveal Himself in so many ways. If He had chosen to do it all at once, I honestly don't think we could have stood it.

Finally around 9:00 a.m., we found the PICU waiting room and pushed the button on the wall to speak with the nurse. I remember being so scared to press the button. I wanted to be with Kaleb, but did not want to hear what was going to be said to me. A nurse stepped out and asked Tom and me to come back into a small room with her while she went over some 'rules' of the PICU with us. I cannot really tell you anything she said except that Kaleb was in a room, and we could go back to see him. They only allowed two people at a time in his room. She also said that during shift changes and in the event a child was having difficulties, we would be asked to leave. I couldn't think about that right now, I just wanted to be with Kaleb.

Tom and I were taken to the PICU's front desk and introduced to some of the staff. Then I remember walking into Kaleb's room and seeing him lying on the bed hooked up to so many monitors that I had never seen before. Each one had a different purpose, and a display was above his bed with numbers and letters that were all foreign to me. I remember thinking, "Is all this necessary?" I don't remember much more about that day, except family members kept taking turns to see Kaleb. The nurses allowed Mollie to come in and see him for a brief moment.

Kaleb was given a popsicle. He had a small tube beside his bed. It had a plastic device on the end that was about the size of a straw. This tube was a lot like the suction used at a dentist's office. Kaleb loved it. He would call it his 'sucker thing.' Anyone who walked into his room would end up on the receiving end of this 'sucker thing.' He loved trying to suck people's skin with it. This is the way we spent the rest of the morning in the PICU.

Finally, Dr. Jones returned and explained that during the surgery for the blood clot, the doctors had taken a quick peek at Kaleb's shoulder and found that the nerves of the brachial plexus had been pulled completely from the spinal cord. They were still not sure if it was all five nerves or just one or two, but at any rate the blood clot was still there. He was going to start Kaleb on a small dose of Heparin. This medication would thin his blood and, hopefully, dissolve the clot. Dr. Jones was using a small dose, because there was some bleeding in Kaleb's spleen, and he did not want to cause more internal bleeding.

So now we were well into Sunday night, and the grandparents offered to sit with Kaleb the rest of the night and let Tom and me lie down. We laid on the PICU waiting room floor and tried to get a little rest. This was very hard to do. I felt so guilty. I knew I was the mother and should stay right by my son, but I also knew that I was exhausted. I had not slept since Friday night, and if I was going to be of any help to Kaleb I needed to at least rest. I was afraid to go to sleep, not because I thought something was going to happen to Kaleb, but because I was afraid of the dreams I might have. I laid there and decided I would just pretend to sleep to keep everyone happy. Yeah right, I fell asleep praying to God to protect me from my dreams.

Monday morning came, and we spent much of the day just sitting and waiting to see if the Heparin was going to work and if Kaleb was going to bleed internally. Every test came back good, and the Heparin seemed to be working. So surgery was scheduled for Tuesday afternoon to place a metal plate in Kaleb's forearm which had been broken. Everything seemed to be slowing down, and I was finally able to break myself away and take a shower. I felt a new sense of energy and rest. So Monday night came, and Tom and I were assigned a small room outside the PICU with a cot. Reluctantly, I laid down to sleep.

I awoke early Tuesday morning. In those wonderful first few seconds, I didn't remember what had happened. Unfortunately, it didn't take long to come back to me where I was and what had happened. I walked into Kaleb's room to find that he was still doing fine. I sat with him and gave him another popsicle. Then it happened . . . things started feeling funny again. Kaleb wanted to play with his 'sucker thing,' so I handed it to him. He took it in his right hand and then dropped it. I laughed at him and said, "Well, Kaleb, what's wrong?" His eyes widened, and he looked up at me and said, "Mommy, I can't hold it!!" At first, I was unsure what was going on. Was he just kidding me? I thought maybe he was just playing and was going to do something to me. I felt like I was being set up. So once again I handed it to him. He started to cry and said, "Really, Mom, I can't hold it, and I feel funny. I feel like the bed is falling!!" Kaleb uttered some cries and screams and then, "Mom, help the bed is falling!! Am I falling? Something is wrong."

I ran and got the nurse. At first she didn't take me seriously. She said, "Some children get this way when they've been in the hospital a while. "He's probably just feeling a little lazy and tired. It's not uncommon for a child to start wanting you to do things for him." After hearing these comments, I knew I had to get serious with her. I said, "You don't know Kaleb. This is not like him. He is not, at all, the type to just lay still when there is a prank to pull or a toy to play with. This may be normal for some, but this is not normal for Kaleb. Will you please get a doctor to take a look at him?" A patronizing smile came across her face, "I will see what the doctor wants to do." she said, as she walked out. With that she was out the door, and I stayed with Kaleb while my mom went out in the waiting room to get Tom. I was in a hospital full of every kind of medical professional you can imagine, but once again I felt isolated. I was alone with a very sick little boy, who was getting worse by the minute. But I was also with God, a God that was getting ready to show us just how powerful He is.

Tom came back and tried to get Kaleb to hold something in his hand—anything. I kept holding his hand and saying, "It's okay, the doctor will be in here in just a minute, and he'll know what to do." As I was speaking these words, the nurse came in with other nurses. She told us that the doctor had decided to go ahead and take Kaleb down now for the arm surgery. I asked, "Shouldn't he see what is going on first?" She explained that was why they were going to operate now. They would go ahead and put him to sleep, place the plate in his arm, then run some tests while he was there to make sure nothing else was going on. They were not very concerned. So with that, Kaleb was once again taken from us, and we were asked to wait downstairs in the surgical family waiting room.

We waited, still not comfortable with the decision to move ahead with the surgery. But who were we to say? These were trained doctors who knew what they were doing so maybe, just maybe, we were just being overprotective parents. We waited for about 30 very intense minutes, then a young man stepped into the waiting area and called our names. We ran over to him, and what he had to say still gives me chills. He introduced himself and explained that he was the anesthesiologist. Then he softly asked, "Are you Christians?" Of course, we both answered with a very certain, "YES." He began to explain his question, "I am too, and I pray every day before I come to work. I always ask God to help me and to speak to me during my shift to let me know the right decisions to make with each of my patients. I prayed that prayer this morning, and God has spoken to me about your son. I was just about to put him to sleep. Actually, I was just getting ready to turn the last button for him to go to sleep, and God has stopped me. I don't have any idea why, but I cannot, in good conscience, put your child to sleep until we figure out what is wrong with him. I hope you understand." I just started weeping right there. I couldn't fight it. Thank God for this man and his faith. I know God had planned for him to work on the day of Kaleb's surgery, and because of his willingness to ask God for help, he was able to hear God's still, small voice that most of us just ignore. He asked us to go back up to the PICU waiting room, and someone would let us know what was going on as soon as the doctors knew.

We walked up to waiting room with relief but also with panic. We felt relief because this man of God had obeyed the Heavenly Father. We were about to panic, because God knew something about Kaleb's condition that we didn't know, and it was obviously important enough to postpone the surgery.

I had not even sat down when a familiar doctor ran into the waiting room with terror on his face. He called out to Tom and me and said, "There you are. I have been looking everywhere for you. We need you downstairs right now. There is no time for talk, just run!!!" Oh, how my entire body wanted to crumble right there. I honestly did not know if I could run. What was I running to? Should I go to it, or should I run in the opposite direction? Then good sense took hold, and I realized that I must get to Kaleb. I have tried to remember the sprint to the operating room with the doctor, but try as I may, I cannot remember one thing about it. My next memory is walking into a small room and seeing Kaleb lying on a bed with several doctors surrounding him. I pushed my way through asking, "What is going on?" I knew it was not normal for parents to be called back to this sterile environment, so this must be bad. Before the doctors had a chance to answer me, Kaleb looked up at me, and God only knows the terror that was on his face. I have never, ever seen someone so desperate and scared. He could not speak out loud, but he whispered to me, "Mom, I can't breath!!" I looked at the doctors and asked if Kaleb was breathing. They just shook their heads "no." I looked back at my child, and he whispered again, "Mommy, please help me. I can't breath. Please Mom, please breath for me. Do something, I am not breathing." I looked at the doctors for an answer, but there was none to be found. You see, they simply did not know why he wasn't breathing. They asked Tom and me to leave. They told us to say our goodbyes and they would do all that they could. I leaned over my child, who by this time was too weak to even talk. I gave him a light kiss on his forehead and said, "You be good for the doctors, and they will help you. Mom will be right outside, and I will see you in a few minutes. I love you with all my heart." I had no intention of telling my son goodbye. I was not giving up that easily.

Once again Tom and I were sitting alone in room full of people, waiting to hear something from someone about our child. I remember crying so hard that I could not hear or see anything else in the room except for Tom's sobs. We were just one bundled up, broken up, pile of helplessness. We were both praying out loud. We just kept saying, "God, forgive us. Whatever has caused this, please just forgive us." My mind raced with all the sins that I had ever committed in my life. What was it? What was I missing? Oh, if only God would just let me know which one it was, I would drop to my knees and beg forgiveness. Then I felt a very light touch on my shoulder. I looked up to see a lady, who had such a sympathetic look on her face, that she almost made me feel better just by standing there. She said, "I don't mean to interrupt you. My son is here for a very simple procedure, and my pastor is here with us. Would you mind if he came over and prayed with you?" I did not ask what church she attended, what their beliefs were, or anything, I just said, "Yes, please, we need prayers fast. My son is in big trouble, and the doctors don't know why." With that, a very nicely dressed man walked over and knelt in front of Tom and me and prayed. I don't remember what he said, but a calmness surrounded us. I felt like I could breath again. I remember just sitting there with this nice lady's arms around me and listening to the most beautiful prayer I had ever heard. They sat with us for a while and then left with a promise to keep praying and to return to check on us before they left the hospital.

Our family came in about that time. Looking back on it, I think God kept them away long enough for Tom and me to get ourselves together so we could calmly let them know what was going on. Again we waited and waited. Finally, Dr. Jones came in. He explained that Kaleb had bled through the small openings in his spine where the nerves were pulled out, and this had caused a blood clot inside his spinal cord at his neck. An orthopedic doctor had been called in, and they were going to do everything they could to remove the clot and save Kaleb's life, but we needed to prepare ourselves for a very long night without a lot of hope.

Chapter 3

Strength from Above

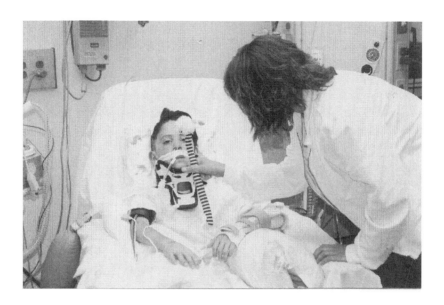

It was somewhere after 4:00 p.m. on Tuesday, June 3rd, and all of a sudden we started getting visitors. Friends and family poured in from everywhere. No one knew what had happened that day. There had not been time to make phone calls, but God knew. He had made the call to our friends' hearts and told them we needed them. They had listened just as the anesthesiologist had listened. We told them all the story of how this one man had saved Kaleb's life, simply by listening to God. If he had put Kaleb to sleep, the doctors would not have known about the blood clot, and Kaleb would have died right there in the operating room.

We all said prayers of thanksgiving and pleaded for more help from God. I remember watching other families come and go. Doctors came in to take them back to be with their loved ones. Oh, how happy I was for them, but how I wished it were us going back there. Time started to crawl. I became so cold. I had a blanket from Kaleb's bed, so I wrapped up in it. If only I could sleep, maybe time would pass, and

I would awake to find this was all a nightmare. About that time, an announcement came over the speaker saying, "Would the family of Kaleb Davis please report to the nurse's station." I ran to the nurse's station. I don't know what I expected, but I was surprised to hear the nurse say, "If you will go over to one of the phones on the wall, you have a phone call." I remember thinking, "WHAT? A phone call? I had been praying so hard to hear something from my son. Now, of all times, I did not have time for a phone call!" Reluctantly, I picked up the phone and spoke into the receiver. A voice that I did not recognize asked if I was Kaleb Davis' mother. I told the lady I was, and she introduced herself as a nurse that was in the operating room with Kaleb. I fell to the ground. Right then and there, my legs decided to give out. I could not stand. Cautiously, I asked if Kaleb was okay. She said, "Yes, of course he is okay. You have a son with a very strong spirit. The presence of God is so strong in this room. Never before have I been in a room with a patient like this. We are all praying while this surgery is going on. If we are not helping the doctor, we are on our knees in the corner praying. When one of us is praying the others are working, and when the one that is praying is needed for your son, someone else takes their place in the corner. Why, even the doctors themselves have been on their knees a time or two. Your son could not be doing any better." I remember saying, "Please don't let him die!" She spoke with faith and strength when she replied, "I promise you, your son will not die in this operating room. I know that for a fact. You just stay there, and we will let you know when the surgery is finished so you can come back and be with him."

After another hour or two passed a nurse walked into the waiting room. It was easy to tell we were Kaleb's family, because everyone else had already left for the day. Even the staff at the nurse's station were gone. We were the only ones left. But I must tell you, there were at least 25 to 30 people in that room, waiting with us! Anyway, this lady walked up to me and said, "I am the nurse you spoke to on the phone. My shift is over now, but I could not leave without meeting the family of this young boy. He is truly a gift from God and will be taken care of." So after giving me a hug, she left with tears in her eyes, and I never saw her again. She was one of the many people God had chosen to represent Him throughout our valley.

My sister was there, and bless her heart, she was trying to keep Mollie occupied. She was talking to Mollie about what was going on with Kaleb. She told me later that she had asked Mollie how she was doing. Mollie replied with a flipant, "I'm fine." This concerned Dawn. She repeated again what had happened to Kaleb and that we were all praying he would be fine. Mollie said, "Yeah, I know." Dawn said, "Mollie, would you like for me to pray with you for Kaleb?" Mollie simply asked, "Why?" By this time, Dawn was thinking Mollie was in denial about what had happened. She, for the third time, tried to get the point across to Mollie that her brother was having trouble now. The reply that she received is a lesson we all need to learn. "Dawn, I know what is going on with Kaleb. I understand what you are telling me. I was very scared, but I already prayed. So now, Kaleb will be fine. Do you want to play?"

I walked outside the waiting room in the hall and found the entrance to the surgery department. It was a large door with a key pad that could only be opened if you were authorized to do so. I knelt down at that door and began to pray. It was getting very late by now. I guess it was 10:00 or 11:00 p.m. and I was very tired, so I just told God my fears. I remember looking at that keypad and saying, "God, I am not authorized to go through that door, but You are. Will you please just go in and walk by the room my son is in? I know that if the hem of your garment will just pass over the doorway, Kaleb will be healed. Please just go by! I know we have asked you for a lot in the last few days, and I don't mean to bother you, but I really need you more than ever." I was praying and crying so hard that I lost all sense of time. People were walking by me, and I never even looked up. I said to God, "I can't even pray anymore. I can't even think of anything to say!! This scares me. I should be praying, and I can't even think what I should pray for. Just please help me. I'm scared, God. This time I'm really scared!" At that moment someone came up behind me and put their arms around me. They were holding me very tight, yet it felt so good. I didn't know or even care who it was. I just hoped they would not turn loose, because they were giving me such strength. Slowly, it felt as if they were rocking me much like a mother rocking her child to sleep. I couldn't stand it any longer. I had to know who this was. I turned around to embrace this person, only to find that no one was there. "God? Is that You?" I asked. That's when I heard the Father's voice inside my head loud and clear. I heard Him say, "It is Me. Now don't be afraid, and don't try to pray anymore. There are many people praying for you and your entire family right now. I am here for you. I have already healed Kaleb, just like I promised. You see, you are my child too, and as much as you love Kaleb, I love you so much more. I want to help you for a while. Kaleb will be fine." So I sat there with God.

Only God Himself knows how long we were there. We just sat there rocking, the two of us together in perfect harmony with peace like I have never felt before. I finally remembered that I should be thinking of Kaleb now and not myself, so I asked God how much longer it would be until we heard from the doctor. As I asked this question, I heard my sister's voice. "There you are! We've been looking everywhere for you, the doctor is in the waiting room." I don't know how that doctor got by without me seeing him. Either I didn't see him while I was taken away with God, or he used another door to exit. Neither of these answers would surprise me.

I remember walking into the waiting room and seeing a circle of people surrounding a very tired, pale, and utterly exhausted doctor. You see, by now it was 12:00 a.m., Wednesday morning. He introduced himself as Dr. Adam Reeves, and said Kaleb was out of surgery and that he had lived through the procedure. However, that was the only good news he had. Kaleb had suffered the exact same injury as Christopher Reeves, the man who played Superman. After Christopher Reeves' accident, he was left paralyzed from his neck down and required ventilation to breath. "That is what we have left with Kaleb." he explained. "I had to partially remove four of his vertebrae starting at the base of his skull to get to the blood clot.

I was able to remove the clot, but he is left with only half of each vertebrae. He will not be able to move anything from the neck down and will require ventilation for the rest of his life. I know this is a shock." I could not hold back any more. I remember pointing a finger in the air and saying, "Oh, no, he won't!" The man was very kind and sympathetic, but he explained that I should prepare myself. It was not a question of *if* or *maybe* but a certainty, because he had seen the damage to Kaleb's spinal cord with his own eyes. This was a permanent and definite diagnosis. I looked around the room at the astonished look on our family and friends' faces. I knew right then and there something had to be done, so I began to speak.

"I want to thank each of you for coming tonight. I love you with all my heart. But I am here to testify that my son will walk again, and he will breath on his own. We do not have to accept this. I want each of you to agree with me on this. If you cannot, I certainly understand and ask that you just go home and pray. I will not think any less of anyone who cannot agree with me at this time, but you will see. Kaleb will walk and talk and be very normal again." Not one person left the waiting room. Everyone stood there in agreement. The doctor said for us to try and rest, and he would be back as soon as possible in the morning to see Kaleb.

We were all just standing there not really knowing what to do next, when, all of a sudden, in walked the lady who had her pastor pray with Tom and me earlier. She was carrying several boxes of pizza and said she thought we might could use something to eat. She told us that her son was doing good, and she had gotten him to sleep. When she realized we were still here, she thought we might be hungry. We filled her in on Kaleb's condition, and she said, "From the first time I saw the two of you pray in the waiting room, I knew your son would be okay, but I have been praying for God to comfort you until Kaleb is back on his feet." How does God do it? I mean, how does He know exactly when to send someone and exactly who to send? I don't know and will probably never know, but rest assured, if you are in a valley someone will be sent to help you make it to the top of the mountain.

A mere six hours later, we were sitting in Kaleb's room in the PICU. It was now 6:00 a.m., Wednesday morning, and Kaleb was starting to wake up. He had a ventilator that was basically breathing for him, but he was awake and knew where he was. With a breath of hope and a prayer of faith, Tom and I asked Kaleb if he could feel us touch his feet. He could not talk, but shook his head yes. The nurse was in the room with us, and she started to cry. I have to admit, even after my big speech about how Kaleb WOULD walk again and not accepting anything less, I was moved with relief. This is about the time Dr. Reeves walked into the room. He looked at us with the same compassion he had just a few hours earlier and asked how we were doing. Tom said, "Doc, we got something to show you." He slowly moved the covers off of Kaleb's legs and asked him to wiggle his feet for the doctor. Kaleb not only wiggled his feet, but actually picked them up and kicked them. The doctor had very large tears in his eyes as he shook his head and said simply, "Awesome, Awesome.

This is unbelievable." He slowly walked out the door and said, "God has been with this child and heard your prayers. I will be back later to check on him."

The days passed and Kaleb became more aware of what had happened. It had been almost a week, and he had not eaten a thing. He had started to loose a little weight, and with the ventilator in place it was obvious that he would not be eating for a while. Dr. Jones ordered a feeding tube to be placed in Kaleb's stomach. The ventilator was in Kaleb's mouth, but he had learned to speak a little bit over it. This was a good sign that soon he would be breathing on his own, and it would be removed. We did not know how long this might take, so the feeding tube would be placed through his nose and down the back of his throat into his stomach. His nurse for the day was the same one he had the first day in PICU. She came in and explained that the procedure, although common, would be very painful for Kaleb. We were very honest with him about the pain he might feel, but that it was necessary. He did not protest. After instructing Kaleb on what she needed him to do, she began pushing this tube into his nostril. It went in fairly easily, and she apologized for hurting him. Kaleb looked up at her and said, "Don't be sorry. Thank you for helping me." She, like Dr. Reeves, was moved to tears and just left the room.

Time started to take a toll on me and the rest of the family. We were all exhausted. Phone calls came pouring in, cards started stacking up, and more visitors arrived than we could count. Every time our pockets were empty, a card would be sent or a visitor would come with money. At first, we started a notebook to list everyone who called, came by, or sent gifts, but after a couple days we had several pages filled and realized this log would be impossible to keep. So we just thanked God for our friends. Prayer chains went up all over our county, and honestly, all over the world. Much thanks goes to WKSK radio and the *Jefferson Post* for running the story about Kaleb. A very, very special thanks is due Mike Powers, who stayed on top of things and kept everyone up to date on our situation. But I must be honest, it was not until I came home that I really saw how much had been done.

One day I was walking into the PICU waiting room alone. I had been downstairs to grab a bite to eat and was going back to be with Kaleb when I saw a couple that had been at the hospital for a while. They were from a different country, and I noticed they always ate in the kitchen part of the waiting room. God put in on my heart to give them some money to go out and eat. But I didn't have any money in my wallet. I had just spent the last dollar I had on a diet Mountain Dew. But again God said, "Just give them what's in your wallet." So I looked inside and there was a $20 dollar bill. I knew this money did not belong to me. It must belong to God, and He had asked me to share it. So I walked up and gave it to the woman and said, "God asked me to give you this. Please don't be offended, just use it for whatever you see fit." She thanked me and took the money. I saw the couple again several days later, and she told me how she had seen fit to spend that $20. "We are from a small community in South America. The money you gave us will feed several orphaned children. I hope you don't mind, but we sent the money to them. They meet every day in the center of our village to pray. Today, they pray for Kaleb Davis! God will touch him!" I know one thing for certain, God not only touched Kaleb Davis, but He sure touched a lot of others too.

Kaleb stayed in good spirits, but sometimes he battled depression. Never, not even one time through it all, did he give up his only defense—prayer. Every time someone would come into his room and ask if he needed anything the answer was always the same, "Do you think you would have time to pray with me?" From the neurosurgeons all the way to housekeeping, not one person refused this humble request. You see, Kaleb did not ask for pain medication, food, drink, or anything else—just prayer. I do believe that God spoke to my child and let him know what it would take to get better. This was a lesson we all had to learn. So the days passed and everyone kept praying.

Home was two hours away. Tom and I had not been back since the accident. Our community, though small in size, is big in heart. Nearly everyone had taken interest in Kaleb and his recovery. The people of Ashe County had come together in one mind and one accord to pray for my son. As I stated earlier, Mike Powers at the radio station, had kept in touch with us and covered Kaleb's story during the news reports. We were, and still are, blessed with good friends and a supportive community.

News spread quickly, and we started getting cards from people we had never even heard of before. People came from all over the state to meet us and pray with Kaleb. Remember the security guard that knew exactly where my child was when we arrived in Winston? He came by and explained the reason he knew was because he too had prayed with Kaleb before we got there. Kaleb had made an impression on this man, and he felt the Holy Spirit's presence around Kaleb, so he, too visited us frequently. Now, remember I say all this not to make it seem like Kaleb is special in any way. It is nothing any of us did, nor do we consider ourselves a chosen family of God. No, quite the opposite. We were so weak that all we had was God, and so we chose God.

I remember being so tired when I would come in to see Kaleb, that I would walk two doors down and go into the wrong room. Every day I would do this. Thankfully, there was not a patient in this room, or I would have walked right in on them. The nurses would laugh at me and say I was too stressed, but I could not stop myself from going into the wrong room.

CHAPTER 4

The Valley of the Shadow of Death

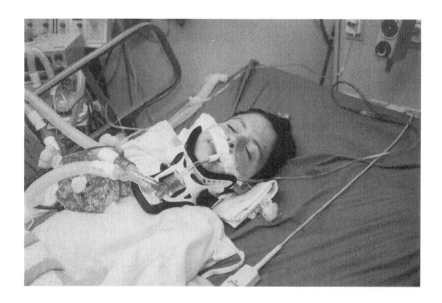

Now that the blood clots in Kaleb's shoulder and spine had both been taken care of, the doctors main concern was to stabilize the vertebrae to prevent paralysis. The decision was made to place Kaleb in what is called a halo. It has small pins that screw under the skin and rest on the skull with a 'halo' around the top. Two pins come down from the halo at the shoulders and hook into a vest that the patient wears. The doctors wanted Kaleb to wear this 'halo' for six months and then it would be removed. This would give the vertebrae time to fuse together. However, Dr. Reeves was going on vacation and would not be back for a week. It was decided that we should not wait, one small incorrect movement of Kaleb's neck, and he would be paralyzed.

So on Tuesday, June 10, exactly one week after the spinal cord surgery, Kaleb was taken to the operating room again. This time they were finally going to put the plate in his arm and put the halo in place. We waited in the PICU waiting room. This surgery did not take long at all. After a couple hours the phone rang, and I thought it would be someone to tell us how Kaleb was doing in surgery. So I answered and heard a voice on the other line explaining that the entire procedure was completed. Kaleb was okay and on his way back up to the PICU. But I heard something else in the tone of the woman's voice—something was amiss. I asked her, "What is wrong?" She said, "Nothing is wrong. Like I said he is okay and he will be upstairs in just a few minutes." I insisted again, "What is it that you are not telling me?" She became a little aggravated with me at this point and said, "He is on his way upstairs right now. You can see for yourself. We always use the term 'okay' when we talk to a patient's family. It simply means he is okay." I hung up the phone with a gut-wrenching feeling that something was not 'okay.'

Tom and I went back into Kaleb's room to wait for him. In just a minute or two in came the nurses pushing the bed that held my child, followed close behind by the ventilator that was once again breathing for him. The halo was a little scary at first to look at, but I kept telling myself it was for his own good. Still, what was this nagging feeling in the pit of my stomach?

The nurse came in and checked Kaleb's eyes with a flashlight. She walked over to the sink and laid down the light and started to wash her hands. It ran through my mind, *Please check his eyes one more time. Something is not right.* I had no sooner finished my thought when she picked up the light, looked puzzled, and walked back to Kaleb. She checked his eyes again. This time she threw the flashlight to the floor and ran out yelling for the doctor. My blood ran cold. I kept thinking, *I knew it. I knew it. Something is not right.*

The next few minutes is a blur. People were running in and out, machines were being hooked up, and a nurse literally jumped up on Kaleb's bed with what I would call a hand held ventilator. She kept pumping this machine with all her strength. I realized she was breathing for my son. The bed he was in was a special one that had an air mattress; it was pumped up by a motor attached to the bed itself. This bed usually took at least two people to push, due to the weight of the motor. Kaleb's nurse began pushing this bed by herself, down the hall, with Kaleb and the other nurse on top. I don't know how she did it, but she sprinted down the hall to the CAT scan room pushing this bed by herself!

Tom and I were asked to wait in Kaleb's room until they figured out what was going on. The only thing they were telling us was that Kaleb was in trouble. They were losing him quickly, but they would continue to do all that they could. I remember lowering my head and praying. Tom jumped up and ran out to the waiting room. All he could say to the grandparents was, "Pray now. Get everyone you can to pray." Phone calls were made and before long prayer chains were going up all over our county like I have never heard of before. As I opened my eyes after praying, I saw that the door to Kaleb's room had been shut, the curtain in front of the door pulled, and several nurses and the chaplain were all gathered around me. I was so scared I was numb. I just kept saying, "He'll be okay, I know he will. You all have to believe me. You all have to have faith. Please don't for one second accept this. Please don't think about him dying. Just feel the Spirit of God and know that He is with us now. Kaleb will not die." Tom just sat there. He looked so pale and helpless. Finally, he got up and said, "I've got to get out of here. Laneice come on." I just looked at him strangely and sat there. He said once again a little louder this time, "I said, come on! Now!" So I got up and followed him.

We walked over to the small room where they take families for consultation. Our parents were in there already. We were hit with dozens of questions to which we had no answer. We all just sat there. Then something happened. Tom looked at me with a look I cannot explain. He looked me right in the eye and said, "I want you to go back in there and tell them when Kaleb is brought back, I want him in another room." Again, I just sat there trying to sort out what was going on. It seemed like the room was spinning out of control, and all I could do was sit there and hold on. Tom stood up and looked at me and said, "I told you what to do. Kaleb will not be brought back into that room. There is death in that room, and I will not have him in there." I don't think I need to tell you that, at this point, I really thought my husband had finally snapped. The pressure was just too much for him, but if it made him feel better I would obey his wishes.

I walked back into Kaleb's room to see the nurses and chaplain right where we had left them, with tears streaming down their faces. They looked up at me, and I explained what Tom had said. Their mouths nearly dropped to the floor. The head nurse said, "This is not a problem. Tell your husband that Kaleb will be moved, if he comes back up."

When I went back in the waiting room with our parents and Tom, there was complete silence. We all just sat there, and the only thing that could be heard was an occasional sniffle or sigh. We were all too exhausted to even speak. That is when Dr. John Miller walked into the room. Dr. Miller was our favorite of all Kaleb's doctors. He was one of the PICU doctors and was an older man that had been a doctor for a while. Everything he told us might happen usually did. We had grown to trust him. He looked at us and said, "I wish I could tell you something for sure, but I can't. All I can tell you is that I suspect a blood vessel may have been struck by the pin of the halo and has caused a blood clot. Kaleb has been sent for a CAT scan. But I must tell you that if this is true, there will not be a lot we can do. With this type injury, time is our worst enemy. Kaleb would need to be in surgery in less than five minutes of the bleed. This is not possible, because we would need a room ready and a neurosurgeon available. Both of these things would take a while to get. I'm sorry, I will let you know more when I can. Keep praying."

So we did. We just prayed and prayed and prayed. Finally Dr. Jones came in, and said that what Dr. Miller had suspected had indeed happened. The back right pin of the halo had been turned 1/4 turn too far and had struck a main blood vessel causing a clot on Kaleb's brain. But Kaleb had been taken to surgery, and the halo was removed. They had gotten to the clot and removed it as best they could. Kaleb was in a coma, and only time would tell what would happen next. With that, Dr. Jones just turned and left. I remember thinking, *How can he just tell us something like that and leave. What happened to the part where he tells us Kaleb is doing great, and we can see him in a few minutes? What happened to the part where he tells us as soon as Kaleb wakes up from surgery we can go home? What is going on?* I just kept trying to sort all of this out. Everything was happening so fast, and I was not prepared for this. As if on cue, Dr. Miller walked into the room. He sat down with us and talked. He just talked. I can't tell you what he said, but just his presence made me feel at ease. I do remember him asking if we had any questions. I looked up and asked the only question that was important to me at the time, "Can you tell me my baby won't die?" He just looked down and said, "I can't tell you that now."

We all just kept sitting there and finally the nurse came in and said, "Kaleb is in his new room, and you can come in now." She led us back through the PICU and into the exact room I had been going to for the past few days! We just walked in and listened to the beeps of the machines and air from the ventilator being pumped into Kaleb's lungs. He just laid there. He had bandages on his head and we were told that the next few hours were the most critical. These were the hours that would determine if his brain would swell or if another clot would develop. So again, we felt alone in a room full of people.

That evening Kathy Blevins, a nurse that always cared for Kaleb at night, came to work. She was our favorite, and we had grown very attached to her. She was special, not only to us, but to Kaleb as well. He would always do better when she was there. They had developed a relationship that was based on their faith in God. Kathy had sat up all night long with Kaleb many times, and prayed with him. She walked in the night after we had the halo experience, and looked at us and said, "I hear you guys are the talk of the unit." I just kind of shook my head and said, "Yeah, it has been a really hard day. We just about lost him." She just laughed and said, "I'm not talking about Kaleb. I am talking about Tom. How did he know to move Kaleb out of the first room he was in? And how did you know, Laneice, all those days ago that Kaleb would be in this room?" We just sat there and let everything sink in. Then Kathy went on to say that the room Kaleb had been in was nicknamed by the unit 'the room of death,' because about 90 percent of the patients that pass away in the PICU, died in that room. And out of that percent, a great many were due to freak accidents. There was nothing in that room that God could not overcome. He certainly did not need Kaleb moved out of the room to save his life. But somehow, I think that He allowed this to happen to show Tom and me that He was with us and that we should listen to Him.

Days and days went by. We sat with Kaleb and waited for him to wake up. Doctors would come in by teams and tell us there was nothing left to be done. They said there was a good chance that Kaleb would remain in this state for the rest of his life. Again, prayers went up.

One particular Sunday stands out in my mind. We had been told that all the churches in our county had decided to have a special prayer service for Kaleb. At 11:00 a.m., they were all going to gather around their altars and pray for Kaleb. We asked the nurse if we could have just a few minutes alone, at this time, to pray with our county over Kaleb. She agreed and walked outside the door. In the PICU, the entire wall facing the hallway is made of glass. As she left she pulled the curtain across the sliding glass door for our privacy. Tom and I stood over Kaleb's bed and prayed. We stayed this way for about 10 minutes and then decided the nurse should come back in. So I went over to pull the curtain to let her know we were finished. I am still moved to tears at the scene I witnessed, when I opened the curtain. The hall was lined with doctors, nurses, housekeeping, and therapists. They were all on their knees praying with us. Only God knows how this touched me.

Every day the same old thing would happen. Doctors would come in and talk without me hearing a word they were saying. Then as they left, I would always ask the same question, "Can you tell me my baby is not going to die?" Every day and every doctor would answer the same way, "No, there is no way we can tell you that now."

By this time, we had been at the hospital long enough that we had a room at the Ronald McDonald house. This is much like a bed and breakfast. It is only for families with children in the hospital, and the cost is simply a donation. Although I was very grateful for a bed, I hated going there because it meant leaving Kaleb. We took turns with our parents going to the Ronald McDonald house to sleep. Tom and I usually went over at 11:00 p.m., and returned to the hospital around 6:00 a.m. the next day. Our parents took turns staying with us at the hospital. The set of grandparents that had stayed up with Kaleb would either go over and sleep during the day at the Ronald McDonald house or return to their home in Ashe County. This team work went on for weeks.

Bob, Tom's father, had retired a few years earlier. Alene, Tom's mother, had just retired in May, right before Kaleb's accident. They would come back home every other day to take care of their own households, then return to sit with Kaleb. While home, Bob and Alene would make sure things at our house were in order. Buck Davis, Bob's brother, mowed our lawn while we were away. Mark Shepherd, a close family friend, would come over every day and feed our pets. Both my parents were still employed full time. However, Linda, my mother, worked at a day care center that closed during the summer months. Bill, my father, worked for a grocery store chain that allowed him to be off whenever he chose. My mother stayed pretty much around the clock with us, only going home once or twice to check on things. My dad had to come home regularly to go to work. It was a difficult time for our parents. They were torn between being with us and making sure their other children were okay. We are all very close, and our family comes before anything else.

One night while walking over to the Ronald McDonald house, I remember looking down at my feet and thinking to myself, "Of all the steps my feet have taken in my life, these are the hardest." I asked God, "Will you please just lighten my steps?" Those were my exact words spoken to God. The next morning we met with some of the doctors. We were told that one of Kaleb's test results were back and things were looking up. I can't even remember what test it was or what it meant, but it was a glimmer of light in a dark valley. I walked out to tell the good news to some family and friends that were in the waiting room. As I was going down the hall another one of the doctors stopped me and said, "You look like you have some good news to tell." I explained about the test results and how I was going to let everyone else know. He looked at me and I'll never forget what his exact words were, "Well, I could tell. It looks like someone has lightened your steps today." I said a silent prayer of thanksgiving and went to spread the good news. This is just one of the many times God revealed Himself by using people who did not even know they were speaking words for God. How many times do we say things without knowing that God is using us? Or worse, how many times do we keep quiet when God wants us to speak?

On another occasion, I was outside and started talking to a nurse who worked at the hospital. She was telling about how tired she was and that she worked in the O.R. and had been having a hard day. "Hang on, your work is not in vain. Because of people like you, my son is alive," I said, trying to let her know she was appreciated. She began to ask what had happened to Kaleb. I started the story and she interrupted me. "Is your son the little boy that the tree limb fell on? Did he have the halo incident?" "Yes, that's him," I confirmed. She said, "I have worked at the hospital for several years, and have never experienced anything like I did the day they discovered the blood clot on your son's brain. When he was taken for the CAT scan, and the doctors realized what was going on; they all but gave up, because they had only minutes to react. Just as Dr. Jones was leaving the Imaging Department to go get you and your husband, he bumped into a neurosurgeon who had just finished up a case in the room next door. Dr. Jones asked if he would help with Kaleb. So Kaleb was pushed into a room that was already set up for brain surgery; all of the equipment needed was in place. I had not even put the drape on your son when the halo was off and the removal of the clot had started. I really don't know how they got to that clot as fast as they did. It is nearly impossible for this to have taken place." I just smiled and said, "I do. God was with us." She returned my smile and said, "Amen." I never saw her again.

Kaleb had been in a coma for at least a week and I had exhausted myself with prayer. I had not slept and had lost about 20 pounds. I felt guilty for not being with Kaleb night and day, but I also felt guilty for not being with Mollie. She was a trooper. She was passed around from family members to friends, and some people she had just met. The poor child really never knew where she would be laying her head down to sleep at night. Through this entire ordeal and to this day, she has never complained. She rejoices in Kaleb's recovery and has prayed as hard as anyone during our trials. I thank God every day for the strength He gives to me through Mollie.

One particular day, I was thinking about all that we had been through and how hard it was on everyone. Okay, I admit I became angry. I was angry at the situation, but most of all I was angry with the doctor who had placed the halo on Kaleb. I had just found out he was a resident and had not completed his training yet, so I became very upset. I went to God in prayer and told him how mad I was. I said, "God, just look at what they have done to my son. Because of their carelessness, Kaleb is in a coma and will never be able to play football again! I cannot believe they let a resident place the halo on him or how careless they have been. Can you possibly imagine how mad I am? Look at what they did to my son!!" A very understanding Father answered me and said, "Yes, I can imagine, and I understand your anger. Look at what was done to my Son. And worst of all, you are the reason it was done! I forgive you and love you. Can you forgive this doctor?" I don't think I have to tell you, that from the bottom of my heart I have forgiven this man, and I wish him nothing but the best. If God can forgive a deliberate and spiteful world that would kill His Son on purpose, nail Him on a cross, and mock Him while He died; I can forgive an accident.

As I said earlier, the support of our friends and family was overwhelming. One day we got word that some dear friends were planning on doing a fund-raiser for Kaleb. They called and asked our permission to have an auction. I remember thinking how nice it was of them to do this, but at the same time I felt unworthy. These people were very busy, and I know money is sometimes hard to come by, so I did not want to impose. Everyone really wanted to do this, so we agreed. It touched me so much, and I could not believe how blessed we were. When you are in a big town, you meet a lot of people. We seemed to be the only ones there with the type of support the good people of Ashe County offered. The other families we met at the hospital could not believe all of the cards, phone calls, and visitors we had; and now an auction? What more could we ask for?

The day came for the auction, and Tom decided that one of us should attend. I told him to go, because I had already made a promise to Kaleb that I would not return home until he did. We were now into the month of July and Tom and I had not been back home. My sister was planning on going to the auction also, and I asked her to take her cell phone with her, so I could call and make sure Tom made it okay. As I went outside the hospital to call her, my cell phone rang. I answered and heard Dawn's voice on the other end. She was at the auction in the gym at Ashe County Middle School. She said, "I have waited in line for a long time just to get in." She was in tears as she described the scene, "Laneice, you wouldn't believe it. There is not standing room in here. I have just watched two cakes sell for $200 each!" I started crying and said, "Dawn, do me a favor. Go up to the stage and tell them to stop. They have done too much. I am afraid someone will give money they need. Don't let them spend their money like this for us. Go and stop them!" The only thing she could manage to say was, "I couldn't stop them if I tried. They want to do this. One man just bought a pocket watch for $100 and then handed it back and asked the crowd to bid on it again."

As if this wasn't enough, a few weeks later there was yet another auction. This time it was held at the ball field in Lansing, our hometown. There were raffle tickets sold as well as items auctioned. I probably, still to this day, do not know what was done for us. I am still amazed and unworthy of this selfless act of kindness. I could never repay the debt I owe to everyone, but I have a Father who is keeping score. I rest assured the debt will be repaid by Him. May God give each and everyone who helped us a special blessing. I pray for the kind of happiness and peace that only He can give, to all those who helped.

Chapter 5

Touched by an Angel

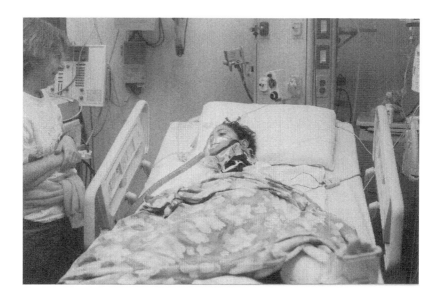

Minutes turned to hours, hours turned to days, and we sat and waited. Every morning several teams of doctors would come in and do the routine checks, explain what tests would be run, then ask if we had any questions. My question was always the same, "Can you tell me my baby will not die?" Every time I asked this question the response was the same. Heads would drop, sympathy would wash over their faces, and with a whispered "no," they would leave. I wanted so badly to hear a "yes." This went on for days. I could not see an end to it. What time I was not asking for the "yes" from the doctors, I was either praying or sitting beside Kaleb's bed reading the Bible to him. I kept talking to him as if he were awake. I told him stories and talked about the special memories we had. I went over all the "remember whens" and the "wait till you get homes." Then we would read the Bible. Every single day was the same. Then every night, Tom and I would take the long walk back to the

Ronald McDonald house to sleep as much as we could, and get up the next morning to start again.

We needed things from home, so Dawn volunteered to go to our house with a list of things we needed. She took Mollie with her. Later she told me that when she walked into our house, a sadness filled her. There laying on the kitchen table was Kaleb's baseball uniform. As most boys do, he had just walked in and thrown it down on the first available place. His cleats were laying in the floor with dried mud underneath them. She walked into Kaleb's bedroom to find his covers in a heap at the foot of his bed and the sheets all twisted. There were toys laying all over the floor. His room was filled with his spirit. Obviously, she could not bear to stay in his room long, so she went around the rest of the house gathering the items on our list. Mollie had been with Dawn the whole time, but she turned and did not see Mollie. Dawn found her in Kaleb's room lying on his bed crying. She had straightened up the covers on the bed and had bundled up in her arms a load of Kaleb's treasures to take back to him. She looked up at Dawn and said, "These are some of Kaleb's things that I know he loves. Can we take them to him?" Needless to say, that little bundle came to Winston with all the other things we had requested.

On one night in particular I could not sleep. I had tried everything, and finally stepped outside and sat on the porch at the Ronald McDonald house to pray. I started out with the same prayer I had been saying for the last month. Then something happened. I could not speak anymore. I could not think, could not talk, couldn't really do anything, but just sit there with my eyes closed. That's when God spoke to me. His voice was loud inside my head and I could hear Him so clearly, "I can hear you. I've been hearing you and I have not forsaken you. Do you trust me?" He asked. I thought about this question for a while. After all this was God talking to me, and He already knew my heart more than I did. So I answered as truthfully as I knew how, "Yes, God I trust you. I know that you can heal Kaleb, but I also know that I need to have faith. Sometimes I get scared that I don't have enough faith. What if I don't have enough faith for you to heal him? What if my faith is not strong enough?" His reply was lovingly placed in my heart. He simply said, "I did not ask about your faith. I simply want to know, do you believe I can heal your son?" "Oh, yes, of course I believe you can heal him. I know that with all my heart. You are able." I was almost shouting praises to Him. Then He interrupted me and said, "Then stop trying to have faith in your faith and let me heal him." This is something to stop and think about. If we believe God can do something, is that not all He asks of us? Sometimes we try to do God's work for Him. Remember the scripture, "Be still and know that I am God" (Psalm 46:10). Oh, how wise our Father is. And how He can put things in our hearts so that we can understand them.

I completely turned things over to God at that moment. I mean I *really* turned them over to Him. I simply knew that even if Kaleb died, God would still be there. Nothing could take away that assurance. So I said to God, "He is yours. I am out of this. I only ask you to help me get through whatever may happen. If you heal Kaleb,

I will go anywhere You want me to and tell about what you have done for us. I will sing your praises to everyone. If you choose to take Kaleb up to be with you, I will still sing your praises and tell everyone what you've done for us." It was just that simple. Come what may, I was going to be okay with the Lord. Then as we were finishing up our time together God said, "I will heal your son and show you my power." I thanked God and told Him I couldn't help still being scared. He understood and told me He would give me help to prove that He was there.

When Tom and I went back to the hospital and entered Kaleb's room, nothing seemed different except for my attitude. Kaleb's vital signs were just as poor as they had been, and he was still not responding to anything. Tom went out for a break during the afternoon and my mom came back and sat with me. I was sitting beside Kaleb's bed reading a book, when I felt someone looking at me. I looked up to see a new doctor standing out in the hall. I just smiled and went back to reading. I could feel the doctor there. He did not move, so I decided to go out and see what he was doing. When I walked out to the hall, I did not see anyone there. I returned to Kaleb's room and looked. He was still there. That is when I realized, the man I was seeing was a reflection, so that meant he was in Kaleb's room! Mom noticed what I was doing and asked what was going on. I told her to look out in the hall. She got up and looked. "Have they called in another doctor?" she asked. "Mom, prepare yourself. That man is not out in the hall. He is in here." She looked at me like I needed a nap. Of course, she walked out into the hall just like I had done. She came back in the room with tears streaming down her face. The nurse had been outside at the station, so she came in to see what was going on.

One-by-one, people started coming into the room to look at this man. All the medical staff saw him—nurses, doctors, and therapists also. Everyone saw the same image. He was a very clean cut man with sandy brown hair, blue shirt, white jacket, black tie, brown dress pants, and brown dress shoes. The picture is still in my mind; it was so clear. One therapist could not believe it; she started turning off lights in Kaleb's room, moving monitors around, moving his bed to a different angle. She even went outside and turned the hall lights off. The man did not move, nor did he change in any way. He simply stood at the head of my son's bed. People from the waiting room started asking to come back and see him. We denied no one. Some cried, some laughed, some just stood in awe and whispered their own silent prayer.

The man stayed there with us for 48 hours. I remember the day he left. I walked into Kaleb's room that morning and looked over in the direction he had been, and he was gone. I said, "Mom, where is he? He is gone!" My mom looked at me puzzled and said, "He was just there a second ago; he can't be gone." But he was. Just as quickly as he had come, he was gone. I wasn't sure how to feel. Why had he left? What did this mean for Kaleb?

Much of the rest of the morning was spent wondering. My sister came down for a visit and so did my dad. Both sets of grandparents were there and some other visitors. With all these people here to see our miracle, why had he chosen this day to leave? I sat in the waiting room with everyone, while my dad was spending some alone time with Kaleb. We were all just sitting around talking when, all of a sudden, Katrina, the nurse for the day, came running into the waiting room. She was smiling from ear to ear and was extremely excited, but that did not stop panic from pulsing through my veins. You never want to see your child's nurse running into the waiting room yelling for you to come quick. All of us stood up to run back to Kaleb's room. When we reached the door, we realized that only two people were allowed back; my dad was already there so just one of us could go. My mom quickly said, "You're the mother, you should go first." I started to run back and looked at Tom. I looked at the nurse and asked, "Could both of us go and let my dad leave when we get back there?" Her answer really was not going to change the fact that I was prepared to fight to the end to be the one to go back to Kaleb. However, she was very excited as she said, "Oh, all of you can come back. This is too good for anyone to miss!!"

We all ran back to Kaleb's room, and he was lying there just like he had since the 'halo' accident, but this time it was different. I took a look at him and thought, *Is he smiling?* I took a closer look, Yes! Yes! He was smiling at me. My dad was standing beside the bed sobbing and rubbing Kaleb's hair. Dad did not wait for the nurse to tell us. He said, "Everybody watch this." He turned to Kaleb and said, "Okay, buddy, just like we practiced. Now stick your tongue out at them." Kaleb gave me that sneaky little boy grin I had not seen in three months, and stuck his tongue out at me and even laughed while he did it. I couldn't stop myself from crying as I leaned over his bed. I saw tears fall from my eyes onto his face. I just kept hugging and kissing him. I did not want to stop. My baby was awake! Tom walked over and leaned down and kissed Kaleb too. He said, "Good morning, buddy. Daddy loves you." Kaleb looked at him and whispered, "I love you too, Daddy." I was crying very hard and shouting praises to God.

At this point I realized I was shouting, not just quietly standing there crying but actually shouting. I remembered that I was in a hospital and there were other sick children there, so I stopped myself and tried to remain quiet. But after I had stopped, I still heard shouting. It was not coming from me, but everyone in Kaleb's room, including several doctors, were all praising God.

We rejoiced and Kaleb rejoiced. What a wonderful day. Then what happened next sent a spine tingle all the way down to my toes. I was leaning over Kaleb's bed with Kathy, his nurse for the night, and Kaleb asked the question I will never, ever forget. He said, "Hey, where did that nice man go? You know the one with the white coat on? Mom, he was so nice to me, and he told me I was going to be okay." So that was it. That was why our angel had left. He had done his job. He came into Kaleb's room and tenderly prepared my baby to wake up and give him strength and courage, so he would not be scared. Thank God for these wonderful angels who I do believe also come to our loved ones who pass on. They tenderly wake them up too, the only difference is when they wake up they are face to face with Jesus.

The doctors decided that afternoon to go ahead and remove the ventilator from Kaleb. So just like that, they pulled the tube right out of my son. He was breathing on his own, but we were warned that sometimes they have to put it back. It could take several tries for him to breath on his own, but eventually the tube would be gone.

Sure enough, that same evening Kaleb started having trouble breathing. His oxygen level, which should be around 97-100, had started dropping. The last time I looked it was around 40. The doctor had been paged, and he was on his way to 're-vent' Kaleb. Tom and I were asked to stay out in the hall, while the nurses worked with Kaleb. Kathy was running by and Tom stopped her. She said, "Just relax, and don't panic until you see me panic." Tom asked how we would know when she was panicking. She said, "I will be running around and get very bossy." Right before the doctor got there, Kathy got bossy. But, thank God, they got the ventilator in place and turned down to do as little of the work as possible, requiring Kaleb to do as much as he could. The doctor started to leave and asked if we had any questions. I said, "Now, can you tell me my baby is not going to die?" I could tell he was choking back tears as he said, "It's still too early to say. I'm sorry."

So Kaleb was back on the ventilator, but he was awake. We read the Bible and Tom went out in the truck and found some bluegrass gospel tapes that belonged to Kaleb. We played *The Roten and Arnold Family* and *The Rock Bottom Bluegrass Band* non-stop. Every time the tape would end, Kaleb would get upset. Kaleb has always had a special place in his heart for Wendy Arnold. When he was little, he wanted to go to every revival service where Wendy was singing, so he could hear her.

After all the excitement and breathing problems, it became difficult for Kaleb to speak. He could not speak clearly, so we developed a method of communicating by spelling the words. I would say the ABC's, and when I got to the first letter of the first word Kaleb wanted to communicate, he would stop me. We had a pen and paper, but Kaleb was too weak to write; so we would write the letters as he spelled them to us. Keep in mind that Wendy starts with a W. By the time I had gotten to W, Kaleb would be so upset with me, he would forget what he was spelling. I remember one time I was frantically trying to figure out what he wanted. He was crying, and I was singing the ABC's. He looked up at me, gritted his teeth, and said, "Wendy, just play Wendy!" After that, we would automatically ask if he wanted Wendy's tape on, before we began the ABC's.

It was during this time that we made a very close and personal friend named Ted Reynolds. He was the pastor at Glendale Springs Baptist Church. Some of our family and friends went to Preacher Reynold's church. Reverend Reynolds came one day for a visit. He walked into Kaleb's room and smiled a smile that lit up the entire unit. We all knew instantly that this was a man of God. Just his presence seemed to comfort Kaleb. The bond that the two of them made was from God. They would pray together, talk, and laugh. What a wonderful blessing this man was to us. Kaleb had severe brain injuries at the time; so short term memory was a problem with most things, but not so with "Preacher Reynolds." Kaleb asked for him a lot.

Preacher Reynolds was about as jolly a man as I have ever met. He made a trip down to see us almost every week. He would walk in, laugh, and say, "How's my little buddy?" Kaleb would always light up when he came into the room. Preacher Reynolds told me one day that it had never entered his mind that Kaleb would not recover. God had spoke to his heart and gave him peace, so he knew his "little buddy" would be just fine. Thank you, Preacher Reynolds.

Kaleb stayed on the ventilator for a week or two, then it was decided that Kaleb could probably breath on his own without it. The tube was pulled again and Kaleb did fine. Oh, how much better he looked without this large tube coming out of his mouth, and thank God we did not have to hear that awful noise it made. One morning as Tom and I were sitting by Kaleb's side, the nurse came in and said the doctor wanted to meet with us. We were called into the conference room that we had sat in so many times before—how I hated this room. Dr. Miller walked in and told us how happy he was with Kaleb's recovery. He was doing much better than any of the doctors had ever thought he would. Then with a wide smile he reached over and laid his kind hand on my knee and said, "Mom, I've been waiting a long time to say this to you . . . Your baby will not die." I just sat there and cried.

Kaleb was improving, but every muscle in his body had been damaged. He was very weak and could not do anything except blink his eyes, whisper a word at a time, and shake his head. He could not cough or clear his throat. This was causing drainage to go directly into his lungs. Because of his injuries, he could not feel the tickle that most of us feel when something is in the back of our throat. He had several cases of pneumonia. To get the drainage out of his lungs, the therapist would have to suction Kaleb about every 2-4 hours. This was so tramatic. Keep in mind that in one side of his nostril was the feeding tube which was about as big around as a pinky finger. In the other side was another tube, about the size of a ring finger, which suctioned acid and other 'stuff' out of his stomach. To suction Kaleb, another tube was forced down the side of his nostril with the feeding tube, down the back of his throat, into his lungs, and then it literally sucked mucus out of his lungs. They would sometimes get half a pint of mucus with each suction. It was unbelievable. This was extremely painful for Kaleb, but he could tell when it was time to suction because it would become difficult for him to breath. He would let us know by asking to pray. His prayer was always the same. I wrote it down so I would not forget it. This is what he would pray, "Our most kind and loving Heavenly Father, thank you so much for all you've done for me. Thank you for sending Jesus to die on the cross so we could all go to heaven. Please bless my mommy, daddy, and Mollie. Be with all my family and help everyone that is sick. Now God, I got a little favor to ask. It's time to get suctioned, so please God, help them to get it out fast and try not to let it hurt so bad." Over and over Kaleb prayed this prayer.

For some reason it was very hard to suction Kaleb. Most of the therapists could not get the tube into his lungs; they would only get it to the back of his throat. However, as I have stated before, God always has someone He sends along. In this case, He sent us two therapists—Sara and Charles. They were the only two that ever really got the tube into Kaleb's lungs. We grew to trust them most. Don't misunderstand, everyone was nice to Kaleb, and some were able to get a little mucus out, but when his lungs were full we would always ask for Sara or Charles.

Kaleb grew very fond of Charles. He was a very large black man. In fact, the only thing larger than Charles' muscles was his heart. He was an ex-football player, which was an immediate plus for him in Kaleb's eyes. And, oh, how that wonderful man could pray. Some nights he would come into Kaleb's room just to pray. I wish you could have heard the two of them praise God together. I don't remember a time that Charles suctioned Kaleb that he did not pray first. He would humble his large body down by the side of Kaleb's bed and pray a very heart-felt prayer, and then he would gently lower the suction tube down my child's nostril. Several times, I saw tears in his eyes as did his job.

Finally, we were sent to the acute care unit. It is a step-down from PICU, but still not a regular room. A nurse in this unit gave Kaleb some ice chips. This was the first thing that he had in his mouth since May 31, and it was now well into July. Kaleb loved the ice chips, but the doctors stopped him from having them. They came in the next day and said, "No more ice chips, until we do a swallow study to make sure the ice is going into his stomach and not his lungs."

The swallow study was done, and we found that everything Kaleb swallowed was going into his lungs. Everyone has a small 'flapper' that is over the top of the tube feeding air into the lungs. It closes when we swallow and opens when we breath or cough. Kaleb's was partially paralyzed, or slow to react. When he swallowed something that was liquid, the 'flapper' did not have time to go down and cover the lungs so everything went directly into his lungs. He could not feel this, so he would not cough it up like everyone else does. This meant no more ice chips.

This moment of pleasure stuck in Kaleb's mind. He would cry for hours saying, "I want ice chips, I want ice chips." Over and over, nonstop this went on and on. We would try and explain that he could not have ice chips, but it would not stop him from begging.

Chapter 6

New Friends . . . New Places

On July 16, 2003, we were sent to Charlotte Institute of Rehabilitation. This is located right beside Carolina's Medical Center. It is about an hour from Winston-Salem and three hours from our home in Ashe. An ambulance came to pick Kaleb up and transport him to rehab. This was a great day, but a little scary. We had to say goodbye to a group of people, who had basically kept us going for two and a half months. The goodbyes were sad. Hugs were given, best wishes were made, and a lot of tears shed. Sara was one of the few therapists that could actually suction Kaleb's lungs. She told us that she did not think it was a good idea to go to Charlotte without a trach being placed in Kaleb's lungs just for suction purposes. She explained that they would not do the type of suctioning in rehab that was being done at Winston, and she was really concerned about it.

The trip to Charlotte was a nightmare. We followed the ambulance in our vehicles. Tom and I were first in line, then Tom's parents, and then my dad. We all tried to stay together on the interstate. It wouldn't have been so difficult if the ambulance driver hadn't been going around 85 to 90 miles an hour. By God's grace, we all made it.

When we got to the rehab center we were in for a shock. We were used to immediate care, nurses 24-hours a day in the room with Kaleb, doctors coming in at least three times a day or more, and respiratory therapists suctioning Kaleb every two hours. At rehab, we had a private room with no nurse, except at the one at the front desk, and the doctor had already left for the day by the time we arrived. I remember praying, "Oh, Lord help us. I can't take care of him alone."

Kaleb was very confused. It was a change of scenery, and he could not understand what was going on. He kept yelling at my mom for leaving him at school. He just kept saying, "You said you would get me and you didn't. Where were you? I was looking everywhere." Then right back to "I want ice chips, I want ice chips." The nurse kept trying to reassure him, but it was no use. He was very upset.

Then the respiratory therapist came in. Tom and I explained to him that Kaleb would probably need to be suctioned, because the ride was long and it had been a while since his last suction. He just looked at us and said, "We don't suction here. Kaleb needs to cough, and if I suction his lungs he will never learn to do it himself." Talk about shock. We were not prepared for this. It was a long, long night.

Tom and I stayed with Kaleb during the night. We tried to sleep, but it was so quiet. No one came in that closed, solid wood door. We felt isolated in that room with our son, and even though the nurse was just outside, it seemed she was miles away. I sat and watched every little breath Kaleb took. I was prepared to run outside at any minute, but he really just slept most of the night without a lot of complications.

The next day we met with Dr. Judy Moore. Dr. Moore was originally from Houston, Texas, and worked at Texas Children's Hospital in the brachial plexus unit. God just kept placing us in the path that we needed to go. What a blessing that we had a doctor, who not only would be helping Kaleb to get back on his feet, but had worked with the number one doctor in the southeastern United States dealing with brachial plexus injuries. She told us there was hope for Kaleb's left arm, and she would see to it that Dr. Akhom from Texas saw us. So with one less burden on our hearts, we spent the rest of the day meeting speech therapists, physical therapists, occupational therapists, recreational therapists, and much to Kaleb's dismay—the hospital school teacher.

That night Tom's parents decided to stay up with Kaleb and let Tom and me go to the motel for some sleep. I was a little more than worried but a lot more tired, so we went. At about 4:00 a.m. the hotel phone rang. I was so scared I didn't feel like I could breath. I picked up the phone and heard Alene saying, "I hate to bother you, but we have done everything we can for Kaleb, and he will not calm down. I don't know what else to do." Tom and I raced over to the hospital to find Kaleb in a fit of anger like we had never seen before. He was telling Alene that he hated her and never wanted to see her again. I walked in and he looked sharply at me and said,

"Get out of my room right now. I hope you die and I never see you again. I hate you, I hate you, I hate you."

The nurse was in the room with us, and she explained this was very common with brain injuries. As the brain heals, patients usually become very angry and a lot of times start cursing. "Will this end?" I asked in shock. She said, "In most cases it does, some however do not. Kaleb will though, I can tell." Tom asked how she could tell, and she demonstrated something to us. While Kaleb was lying there shouting out his demands, she lowered her voice and said, "Kaleb, I need you to listen to me." Immediately Kaleb was quiet. He was only quiet for a matter of seconds, but he did respond to her instructions. She told us that the ones, who do not recover, are not able to obey commands. I said a prayer of thanksgiving and spent the rest of the night telling him how much I loved him, even if he didn't think he loved me. Thank God, this only lasted for one night, and then we were back to the never ending, "I want ice chips."

The next morning, bright and early, in walked a very pretty lady. She had light brown hair that was pulled neatly back in a ponytail. She introduced herself as Amanda and told us she would be Kaleb's speech therapist. I looked at Kaleb and said, "You better be nice to Amanda, she is the one who will help you get ice chips." So he decided right then and there to be on his best behavior. He patiently obeyed her every command and continually reminded her that he wanted ice chips. This went on for a few days, and then one day Amanda walked into Kaleb's room, and he smiled a large sneaky smile at her and said, "My Amanda, you're looking ravishing today." She laughed very hard but said this would not get him ice chips any faster than before. But before Amanda left that day, she let him have a few ice chips.

Therapy proved to be very tiring for Kaleb. He spent about an hour in the morning with Ms. Ann, the occupational therapist, an hour with Scott, the physical therapist, then an hour with Ms. Amanda, the speech therapist, thirty minutes in recreational therapy, and then school. Kaleb's teachers at Blue Ridge Elementary in Ashe County would send homework for the week, and the hospital teacher would go over it with him. Kaleb usually fell asleep during this time. This is how we spent the next month and a half at rehab.

Tom and I would sometimes go down to the gym with Kaleb and watch his physical therapy. We did not go every time, because it seemed that he did better without us. Scott started by trying to get Kaleb to hold his head up. He had the neck brace on, and he would rest his chin on the brace so his head would hang down just a bit. Scott would say, "Kaleb, sit up straight. Hold your head up." He would get a mirror and stand it in front of Kaleb and say, "Now, look in the mirror." Kaleb would slowly raise his head and cry, "I'm ugly!" He refused to look in the mirror. He would keep repeating, "I'm ugly, I'm ugly, I'm ugly." Because Kaleb would get so upset at the sight of himself, the mirror was taken away, and we worked on holding his head up without it. This took many weeks, but finally he did not rely so much on the collar.

Preacher Reynolds and his wife, Ann, would come for regular visits and prayer time. They were such a blessing to us. God would usually send Preacher Reynolds at the exact time we needed him. One time in particular was when Kaleb was scheduled for a swallow study. It was going on 90 days since he had been able to drink. If he passed this test, he could finally have some water. He was so excited. He was so thirsty that when I would brush his teeth, he would grab the toothbrush and suck every bit of water he could out of it. People would come in Kaleb's room, and he would tell us they had been drinking Pepsi, because he could smell it on their breath. My heart broke for him. This day was very important to Kaleb.

Dr. Moore came in and gave him some pointers on how to pass the test. "Just try to relax and concentrate on what Ms. Amanda has taught you. You'll do fine." So Tom, my mom, Preacher Reynolds, Ann, and I all walked with Kaleb over to the hospital for the big test. It was awful. The department that administered the test was behind schedule. We sat in the hallway for over an hour waiting our turn. When we were finally called back, the staff was tired and not very patient. The nurse took a large syringe and pushed various liquids down Kaleb's mouth. She was doing it so fast that I don't even think I could have passed the test. We asked her if she could slow down, and she said, "No, I can't!" I stood inside a little room with the doctor and watched a screen that showed exactly where all the liquids went. Everything was going into his lungs. He did not pass the test. We were so discouraged that we cried all the way back to rehab.

Days passed and we kept practicing everything we could to improve Kaleb's swallowing. We also did all the 'homework' that the therapist would assign Kaleb. Despite all the hard work and long days, we still had time to have a little fun. Kaleb was voted the vice-president of the pediatric hall, and our new friend Jackie was voted president. Jackie was 17-years-old and was left paralyzed from the waist down from a diving accident; but what a trooper he was. Not one time did he complain. He made a joke out of everything. He had gotten hold of the x-rays that were taken of his neck. He had them hanging on his window so everyone could see the nuts and bolts that "held his head on." Jackie was great.

Every night there was a party in Kaleb's room. Jackie would ride his wheelchair up and down the hall getting all the children together. They would come into Kaleb's room to watch a movie, eat popcorn, and play the playstation. Jackie would motivate Kaleb to try to play. He showed him tricks to get what he wanted with the nurses. Everyone was happy when Jackie was around. One night he even helped us keep Kaleb awake all night for a test the next morning. This was a test that would tell whether or not Kaleb would need to stay on his seizure medicine. It had to be administered with sleep deprivation. It was oh-so-hard to keep Kaleb awake. Every time Kaleb would start to doze off, Jackie would pop him in the head with a balloon. It was hard, but we did it. Kaleb passed the test, and he was taken off the medication. One down, with about five more to go.

The time came for another swallow study. It had only been a week since the last test, but Dr. Moore felt that kaleb would do better with a different nurse and better scheduling. We went down that same long hallway, with fear in our hearts that he would not pass. After praying long and hard, we went into the test room. I was behind the same wall with a different doctor this time. As the liquid was pushed into Kaleb's mouth, I listened carefully to what the doctor said. I could not tell by looking at the screen where the liquid was going, but I knew it looked different this time. The doctor just kept saying, "Good, Kaleb, now try again." Then I overheard him say to a nurse who was training, "Now see how the liquid goes past the lungs?" I started crying; Kaleb started crying; and the nurses started crying. We all cried! We went out of the testing room and met my mom bringing a bottle of strawberry juice! Kaleb took several sips and then said, "Where's Ms. Amanda? She promised me a Mountain Dew!"

This was one large burden taken off of our shoulders. Kaleb could eat and drink anything he wanted. However, he did not want to eat. We tried everything from fried chicken to chocolate milk shakes, but nothing tasted right to him. Every time he would eat, he would throw up. A lot of times it would be instant. The food would go in, and he would throw-up. This went on for weeks and weeks. Even when we came home it would still happen. Thank God, with lots of prayer, it has stopped. We never really found out why. Many tests were run, but nothing ever showed up. Sometimes, I think these little stumbling blocks are put in our way to distract us. They are placed by Satan and serve no purpose, but to try to stop us from keeping our faith.

I prayed a lot about Kaleb's eating problem. You see, he still had his feeding tube in, and the doctors did not want to take it out until Kaleb proved that he could eat enough to, at least, maintain his own weight. He had not proven this, so at night he would get supplements from the tube. I thought that perhaps, because the tube went down his throat, that when he swallowed, it would wiggle, and activate his gag reflex causing him to throw up. I prayed that the doctors would remove the tube, but they would not. Then one day the tube became stopped up. The nurse worked and worked with it, trying everything possible to get rid of the clog. She looked at us and said, "If this does not clear out, we will have to take the tube out and put in another one." I saw the door of opportunity open wide. I said, "Call Dr. Moore. Tell her it's stopped up, and ask if you can take it out and let Kaleb try to eat without it. We could then tell if the tube is what is causing him to gag."

Praise God, my prayer was answered, and Dr. Moore agreed. There was one condition though, we had to keep a journal of everything Kaleb ate. She would give him a couple days, then if he was not able to eat enough the tube would be placed again. Kaleb ate as much as possible and we wrote down everything!!! I mean everything. His journal looked like this: "Kaleb had two sips of fruit juice." "Kaleb ate one bite of an apple."

I formed a friendship with the security guard at the rehab center. This friendship was, once again, inspired by God. He was a very Godly man with a great faith. He was sick with cancer, but refused to let it defeat him. We prayed many times for each other. Anyway, this friendship allowed me access to the kitchen. We went to the grocery store and bought supplies. My mother-in-law brought some of our pots and pans from home and together we fixed Kaleb some 'good ole fashioned Ashe County country cooking.' He ate better than usual, and Dr. Moore did not make us put the tube back in.

It was well into August by now, and we still had not been home. We continued through rehab in a steady routine. Every day was pretty much like the day before. One day, however, stands out in my mind. I had stepped outside while Kaleb was in the gym with the therapist. He was doing physical therapy with Ms. Kendra, because his usual therapist, Scott, had taken the day off. All of a sudden, Summer Farmer, Brant's fiancé, came out to get me. She said, "Laneice, come in. They want you in the gym." I ran with her to the gym to find all of Kaleb's therapists, two of his doctors, and many of our family looking at Kaleb amazed. There was Ms. Kendra in front of Kaleb, Ms. Ann behind him, and there stood (yes, I said stood) Kaleb. He was holding onto the parallel bars and taking steps. One small step at a time, but a step just the same. We were all laughing, crying, and praising God. After four months of fear, Kaleb and God had proved them all wrong. HE WAS WALKING!

Chapter 7

There's No Place Like Home

Dr. Moore contacted Dr. Akhom in Houston. He agreed to take Kaleb as a patient, so it was decided that the week of Sept. 15, 2003, we would go to Texas and meet the team of doctors who would try to correct the nerve damage in Kaleb's immobile left arm.

Dr. Moore allowed Kaleb to go home on September 5, 2003, to spend a few days there and then fly out to Texas for the first nerve graph surgery. I remember the day when we had to say goodbye to our friends in Charlotte. We were so happy to be going home, but yet we had grown very close to these friends, and it was hard to leave them. As we went through the discharge process, each person we had met came by to give us hugs and kisses. After some tears and "thank you's," we walked down to the entrance of the hospital to wait for Tom to bring the car. It sure was wonderful to be going home.

We loaded everything up. It took our car, my parent's car, and Tom's brother's car to haul everything back. Our caravan was in line once again. We were off; heading straight for Ashe County as fast as our little green Jetta would go! When we pulled out of the parking lot, there was a large poster that said, "Goodbye Charlotte, Hello

Ashe County. Congratulations Kaleb." I remember thinking, how nice the sign was, and Mollie and Kaleb were really excited to see it.

We drove to Statesville, where we had planned to stop at a rest station to meet some of Tom's family. His aunt, Mary Woodie, and his cousin, Tracie, and her kids were all there. Posters were everywhere. They had decorated the station with welcome home signs and pictures they had drawn for Kaleb. Again, I thought, "This is nice! Mollie and Kaleb really enjoyed it.

Down the road we went again. Mollie was sitting in the back seat with me, because Kaleb had a special buckle that only fit the front seat. I looked over at her and she looked so happy. The poor little girl had been through a very tough summer. She had been sent all over the place from week to week and sometimes even from day to day. Although this was very hard on her, and the guilt that I still feel today is undescribable, I am very thankful for those who spent time with her when we could not be there. She was welcomed into many homes.

We had not traveled very far down the road when, all of a sudden, another poster popped up, then another one, and another one. Each one had a different message on it. For miles and miles they would say, "Great Job Kaleb." "Welcome home Kaleb" or "50 more miles."

Kaleb loves the mountains of North Carolina. It is his favorite place on earth. Ever since he was old enough to talk, when we would go to the beach and come home, he would start asking, "When will we see the mountains, Daddy?" Tom would always say, "Just be patient, Kaleb, we will see them soon. I will let you know as soon as you can see them." There is a place just before you get into Wilkes County that you can see the mountains for the first time. Tom would always say, "Look, Kaleb, there's your mountains!" When we reached this place coming home, wouldn't you know it, there was a poster written in big bold letters, "Look Kaleb, there's your mountains!!" Kaleb was looking at the actual mountains that God had created with trees and flowers blooming. But do you know what I saw? I saw the mountains that we had been climbing since May 31. We were finally on top of our 'spiritual mountain.' Do you know what I heard? I heard my Heavenly Father say, "Look, Laneice, there's your mountains."

Special thanks goes to my sister for all her hard work on the many posters. Thanks also goes to Yvette Jones, Cindy Powers, and Erin Greer who helped her put them up. They stayed up until the early hours of the morning placing these posters along the interstate. They went all the way from Charlotte to our front yard. This covered approximately 150 miles! Along with the posters were yellow ribbons that had been tied by Cathy Finley, one of my co-workers. How grateful I was for these beacons leading us home.

I truly had no idea that the good people of Ashe County had been awaiting our homecoming. When we finally got close enough that our radio would pick up WKSK, Tom turned it on, and we started listening to familiar hometown voices. It seemed so good to have that little piece of home in our car. All of a sudden, the program was interrupted by the very familiar voice of our good friend, Mike Powers. He said, "What a beautiful day in the High Country, and what a beautiful day for a homecoming. We would like to welcome home Kaleb Davis and his family. I've just been informed that they have entered into Wilkes County." I was astonished, first of all that they were talking about us on the radio and secondly that they knew where we were.

Wilkes County had never looked better, but in a funny way Ashe County seemed like a lifetime away. We crossed the Wilkes/Ashe County line and tooted our horn. We were so happy. My mom had suggested that we get some posters on our car that said, "Thank you, Ashe County." I made them with supplies we had bought in Charlotte. I didn't really know why we were doing it at the time, but I was so grateful for the support of our neighbors. We stopped out on Highway 163 to place them on our car. We pulled off the road and were attaching them on the doors and tying balloons to the antenna, when an unmarked police car pulled up beside us. I looked at Tom and said, "Oh, no, I bet we aren't supposed to have these on the car." Tom walked over to the police officer and talked to him for a minute. He came back to me and said, "You're not going to believe this. He wants to escort us into town."

He was right, I couldn't believe it. Then I heard Mike on the radio again stating our location and telling people we were getting ready to drive downtown. I was simply not prepared for what we saw. Every door and every window had yellow ribbons and streamers hanging from them. People were standing in the road waving. They were actually hanging out of the second story windows waving streamers at us. As we drove through town, everyone was yelling encouragement to us. All I could do was cry and wave back to them.

As we drove on past Main Street the policeman tooted his goodbye, and in the distance, I saw a fire truck from Lansing Fire Department pull out in front of us with its lights flashing. Oh, I had so much joy and pride in my heart for our community that I honestly thought it would explode. Ribbons were everywhere. Posters were every mile or two. We reached the community of Warrensville, and there were more people lined up, waving, shouting, and crying.

Next, we drove through the Blue Ridge Elementary parking lot, Kaleb and Mollie's school. I was under the impression that Kaleb's class wanted to wave at him as we drove by. Again, what I saw was totally unbelievable. Not only Kaleb's class, but the entire school stood in line up and down the school drive. Some had signs they had made, others had ribbons, but almost everyone had tears of joy. All the way home crowds of people lined the road.

The big red fire truck brought us all the way home. He even pulled right up in our driveway. That is when I saw the driver. It was my cousin, Jeff Venable, and the closest person I ever had to a brother. Our yard was full of family. My dad's sisters had made us a home cooked meal that looked like 'dinner on the ground' at an old fashion baptist church. Oh, how good the food was.

The house itself was decorated with balloons, streamers, and more wonderful posters. The bank that leads up to our back porch had the most beautiful brand new sidewalk. This sidewalk led the way to a very well build ramp, that would allow Kaleb to be wheeled right into the house. We walked in, and the smell of home filled our souls. I don't think it was the cedar logs our house is made of, or the cleaning supplies my dear sister had used to clean our house; it was the smell of love that filled us. This is an odor not made by man, but one sent right straight down from the gates of Heaven and given to us freely by our Heavenly Father! Can you imagine the smell that will fill our souls, when we get to the home He has prepared for us in Heaven?

The only dream I ever had of Kaleb, while we were in Winston, happened the night before we were going to Charlotte for rehabilitation. I dreamed that Tom, Kaleb, my mom, and I were all at an airport. Tom had taken Kaleb to the restroom, so I was waiting with my mom. All of a sudden, Kaleb came running around the corner with a baseball uniform on and said, "Watch this Mom, I can slide." He slid across the floor, and I said, "Kaleb, be careful, your neck surgery has not been done yet." That was all I dreamed, but it was so powerful. It seemed so real that I told Tom I almost believed it to be a sign from God, except the baseball uniform was blue. The little league uniforms had been purple ever since Tom had played as a boy, so I could not figure that part out. Also, why in the world would we be at an airport with my mom? But yet, somehow it all seemed so real.

After we had been home a few days, Danny Farmer called and told us that the little league team had agreed to leave one empty spot on their roster for Kaleb. He could not play of course, but they wanted his name on the roster. They wanted him on the team. He also asked what size uniform Kaleb would need. I told Danny not to order Kaleb a uniform, because he still had the one from last year, and there was no use of wasting money for a new one. Danny insisted on ordering Kaleb a uniform. So I gave him Kaleb's size, and in a few weeks he showed up at our door with a brand new BLUE uniform. He said, "Oh, yeah, they changed the colors this year." God was still giving us signs that would strengthen us.

We were home for about a week, and then we were off to Texas. It was a blessing from God to be going, but it was still a very hard thing to do. Tom, Kaleb, and I had to fly to Texas, and that was a little more than scary for us. Kaleb was still so weak, and all I could think of was, "What if he has complications on the plane?" I did not know for sure how the altitude would effect him with all the injuries he had. But on Sunday, I found myself in a car loaded with suitcases, medicine bottles, and three round trip tickets to Texas. Once again, Mollie had to stay at home. I watched her cry in the rear view mirror until we were out of sight. Then I prayed, "God, please, once again I ask for Your protection for us on the plane and for Mollie at home. And thank You for all You've done and for all that You are going to do."

We arrived at the airport and looked at the very, very long line that awaited us. We were exhausted and scared. Slowly, we wheeled Kaleb through the lobby and took our place in line. We handed the lady our tickets and driver's licenses, she looked at Kaleb and smiled. She said, "You can go around the corner with your son and enter the elevator. It will take you downstairs, and there is a guard there who will show you what to do." We went down and were greeted by a large man in a uniform. He directed Tom and me to the metal detectors and said, "I'll have to take the child into this other room to check his wheelchair." Can you believe that someone would actually place weapons in a wheelchair with a child? What kind of world do we live in?

Kaleb went with the security guard, and Tom and I watched as they scanned him and the wheelchair. Kaleb came out with a very young, slender black man, and I am not sure who was smiling the biggest. Kaleb later explained to us that he and this young man had talked about how good Jesus was. God has chosen people all over this world, if you just take the time to recognize them.

We got through security with few complications, unless you want to count the fact that Tom's shoes had medal in them, and he too had to go into a little room and be 'patted down.' The flight began as normal. We were allowed to sit in bulkhead seats, the front row of the tourist section, because it had more leg room for Kaleb. The stewardess was very nice, and she too had a handicapped son who had been in an accident. So we got some 'special treatment.'

The plane took off and everything seemed to be normal. In the hospital, I had learned to look at the nurses faces, instead of the machines, to see if anything was wrong. I once again used this strategy to see how our flight was going. I watched the other passengers and began to feel at ease. Everyone was talking and laughing, reading a magazine, or just dozing in their seats. "Okay, I thought, this isn't so bad."

Then I started noticing more and more people asleep. Kaleb included. I became very sleepy myself and was just about to drift off, when all of a sudden, I started to feel very funny. The first thing I noticed was that I could not hear as well. It got worse and worse and my head started to spin. I turned to ask Tom if he was okay and did not need to ask. The look on his face told it all. He was scared to death and talking to me, but I could not hear anything. I looked up and saw that everyone was experiencing these symptoms. Panic then struck all of the passengers, including the stewardesses, who began strapping their seatbelts on, ignoring the calls from the passengers. Kaleb continued to sleep. Praise God!

I was trying to move my arms, but they were in slow motion. I could not feel them moving, but I could see them. It was a very strange sensation. Not, however, as strange as the next thing I felt. The plane began to go nose down—FAST! The pain in my ears was almost unbearable. Alarms were sounding and people were crying. "Oh God," I thought, "Why now? Why are we in this plane? What is going on? Are we going to die now?" Thank God, we will go together. Then it hit me. It hit me like a lead ball—MOLLIE. "Oh God," I prayed, "She can't be left alone. Please God spare one of us for her."

It was just about that time that the nose of the plane leveled off, my hearing came back, and Kaleb started to wake up. Everyone was beginning to calm down, when the pilot's voice came over the intercom announcing that we had lost cabin pressure. The loss of cabin pressure causes the loss of oxygen. He apologized for the bumpy road down, but he had taken us from 33,000 feet to 14,000 feet in less than two minutes. We were now below 14,000 feet (the altitude that you can travel without losing oxygen) and we would be delayed, but all would be fine. Isn't it great that, even though, I only asked God to spare one of us for Mollie, He did more than I asked and spared us all?

CHAPTER 8

Listening To God

So we arrived in Houston. We thought Winston and Charlotte were big? Ha! They are nothing to this huge city! We walked cautiously through the airport, found our luggage, and then wondered how we were going to find the cab driver who was supposed to pick us up. We walked over to the exit, and standing there was a very well dressed man holding a sign that read, "Davis Family." We felt stupid when we saw all the other well dressed men holding signs for other travelers. We were inexperienced in the traveling world.

As we drove from the airport we looked around, and everywhere you looked there were roadways; not just one or two lanes, but about five lanes in each direction and two or three roads stacked on top of each other, with bridges carrying passengers over the ones below. *Lord*, I thought, *what on earth are we doing here?* I noticed the cab had slowed down, and I saw buildings upon buildings. I said to the cab driver, "So is the hotel right in the middle of downtown?" It was a city as large as downtown

Charlotte or bigger. He just kind of laughed and said, "Oh, no, this is not downtown, this is just the medical complex." The Texas Medical Center is the largest medical complex in the world. People go there from all over the world for treatment. Can you imagine a city as big as downtown Charlotte that is nothing but hospitals? My heart still breaks to know that there are that many sick people in the world today. We should always remember them in our prayers. A lot of them may not know the Lord.

We checked in the motel and went straight over to the hospital for our first meeting with the brachial plexus team. We met Dr. James Malone. He was what you would imagine a true Texan to look like; a very tall man with a very large hat, and a Texan all the way down to his snake skin boots. He took one look at Kaleb and asked, "Your neck broke, boy?" Kaleb just rolled his large brown eyes up at him and said, "No." So without another word, Dr. Malone reached over and jerked the neck brace off of Kaleb's neck. We all let out a unified breath of fear. He told Kaleb that if he wanted to get better, the first step was to start acting and looking better. Dr. Malone was rough and tough, but we grew fond of him and his direct approach to Kaleb.

Dr. Malone asked us what we had been told about Kaleb's injury. We explained as much as we knew at the time. We had been told that three of the five nerves had either been pulled completely out of Kaleb's spine or at least stretched out. Dr. Malone rubbed his chin, looked at Kaleb and said, "Look up here at me, boy. Let me see your eyes." Kaleb looked up and Dr. Malone just shook his head and said, "Nope, all five are pulled completely out, sorry." I could not believe this. Just who did this jerk think he was? He had not even examined Kaleb. How could he tell? So I got my nerve up and asked him. He said, "I've been doing this a long time. I can tell by the way the patient's eyes dilate. He has all five completely pulled out. But, don't worry, we'll take care of it."

So what else could we do? We went back to our motel, got a little sleep, and arrived back at the hospital at 5:00 a.m. the next morning. Kaleb was taken back to surgery. This was so different from the last surgeries. There was no family, no friends, just Tom and me alone in the waiting room. We anxiously awaited word from someone we did not even know yet.

After about four hours, Dr. Malone walked out to the waiting room. I remember thinking, *Don't take us in a little room. I hate those little rooms.* I guess I was so upset and scared I said it out loud. He just laughed and said, "Why would I do that? I just came out to tell you I'm done and Kaleb is fine. But, (it seemed like there was always a but) I didn't do the nerve graph. He was leaking spinal cord fluid, it probably has been leaking since the accident; so we put a patch over the place. We'll keep him a few days, send him home, and y'all will just have to come back down for the graphing." Then he turned to walk off. I said, "Wait a minute. What do you mean leaking spinal cord fluid? How dangerous is that? What will happen to him? Where is he now? Can I see him?" He just laughed and told me to calm down. Kaleb would be all right; they'd call me in about fifteen minutes and we could go back and see him. With that he was gone.

Thirty minutes had passed and I was getting very anxious. Dr. Malone had said fifteen minutes. I paced the floor with Tom right behind me. We waited and waited. Finally, I couldn't stand it any longer. It had been 45 minutes. I walked up to the nurses station crying. I asked, "Will you please check on my son. I haven't heard from him and his surgery was over 45 minutes ago." The lady called back to the recovery room and repeated Kaleb's name several times, then even spelled it. She hung up the phone and said, "He's not in recovery yet. I can't check anywhere else."

Okay, so if his surgery was over 45 minutes ago and he is not in recovery, where is he? The doctor is gone, so where is my son. I was so scared. I tried to sneak in the operating room, but lost my nerve. I didn't want to cause someone to be distracted from doing their job. Anyway, God was with us. We survived the accident, the hospital, rehab, and that awful plane ride here. God would surely not leave us. So I sat down and prayed.

An hour and a half after Dr. Malone came out, our name was called over the intercom. We went to the nurses station and were greeted by a very sweet smile. The nurse introduced herself as Katie, and said she had been with Kaleb for the last few minutes and had already prayed with him. Yes, God's love is everywhere. There is always someone who is willing to carry out His work.

Katie laughed when I told her Dr. Malone had said it would be fifteen minutes. She said, "I don't know why he always does that. When he came out to talk to you, he was finished with his part, but Kaleb had not even been sewn up. It takes a while to get him cleaned up and stable enough to have visitors. "Besides," she said, "it gave me some time to be alone with Kaleb and God. I don't have to tell you this, but your child has a very strong spirit about him. I can feel the hand of God on him, and it overwhelmed me."

Kaleb had to stay, as expected, in the hospital for about four days, and then we stayed in the motel for our last night in Texas. Then bright and early, we went back to the airport and prayed for a better flight home. As usual, God heard our prayers and granted us a safe flight back.

We came back home, and had to tell the family that we would be going back to Texas in a month to try again for the surgery. Meanwhile we went to therapy, school and church without missing a beat. God had given us so much, we could not possibly let Him down now.

Time passed quickly, and it was time to go back to Texas. It was November 2003, just under six months since the accident; and we were going back to the hospital. This time, my mom decided to go with us. We were in the airport terminal, and Kaleb needed to use the restroom. As my mom and I stood outside the restroom waiting on Tom and Kaleb, I suddenly remembered my dream in Winston. Kaleb had a BLUE little league uniform, and now I was standing in an airport waiting with my mom for Kaleb to come out of the restroom. God simply never stops revealing Himself to us.

Our second trip to Texas was quite different from the first. We got to the hospital, had the surgery, and were called back into the recovery room. Once again we had Katie in recovery. She told us that she saw Kaleb's name on the schedule and told everyone she was pulling rank. Kaleb was her patient. So they had prayed again together before she called us back.

Dr. Akhom had not done the surgery. Dr. Malone went in as before, and located the working nerve in Kaleb's right arm, to be used to help his left arm work. He also located a nerve that runs down the side of Kaleb's left arm that he did not need. This nerve was removed by Dr. Akhom's assistant, Dr. Roten, and attached to the nerve in Kaleb's right arm, stretched along his chest to be attached on the other end to his left arm to replace the damaged nerve. This surgery was finished and everything seemed fine. We were sent back to a regular room and like the first time, stayed for four days, and then returned home.

Time passed and after many visits for routine check-ups in Charlotte, all that was left to do was to wait for the healing of Kaleb's arm. It was time, once again, to focus on the spinal cord injury. Dr. Moore referred us to an orthopedic surgeon, Dr. Kenneth James, in Charlotte. He would look at Kaleb's neck and decide what to do to help it heal to its full potential. Dr. James told us that Kaleb needed yet another surgery on his neck. He wanted to go in and insert medal pins, vertically, down the sides of Kaleb's neck, and then insert smaller pins, horizontally, to connect the first set of pins. He would then graph bone from Kaleb's hip, and attach it to the vertebrae that had been left in his neck. The bones would then fuse together.

The thoughts of this surgery really scared us, especially after the halo accident. We began to pray about it. The more we prayed, the more it seemed God told us it needed to be done. So we decided to wait until Kaleb was a bit stronger and then have the surgery. Dr. James planned on doing the surgery in April 2004.

Meanwhile, we got a call from Dr. Moore telling us that Dr. Akhom had scheduled a clinic in Charlotte, and they would like for Kaleb to see him. It was March, and had been about four months since Kaleb had been to Houston. Dr. Akhom wanted to make sure Kaleb was doing well from the surgery Dr. Roten had done earlier. So we went down to Charlotte hoping that we would find Kaleb's arm exactly where it should be. Unfortunately, we got some bad news. When Dr. Akhom checked Kaleb's arm, he seemed concerned. There was not as much progress as he had hoped. So upon investigating the notes from Dr. Roten, we found out that he did not 'hook-up' all the nerves he was supposed to. He had connected the nerve to the biceps only, nothing else. Kaleb did have movement in his biceps, but no triceps movement and nothing below his elbow.

Dr. Akhom said that time was running out; the nerve needed to be attached as soon as possible. He said, "From now on, I will do all Kaleb's surgeries. No one else will do them. But this needs to be done right away." So the nurse scheduled us for surgery in April 2004. This appointment was a conflict with Dr. James. We mentioned this to Dr. Akhom, and he was pretty firm that we were running out of time. He asked us to check with Dr. James, but to let him know how terribly important it was to do the arm as soon as possible.

Dr. James was not exactly comfortable with the postponement of the spinal surgery. He said he thought Kaleb would be fine, but it did make him nervous to wait. One wrong slip and Kaleb could be paralyzed. What a decision to make. We once again went to the One with all the answers. We scheduled a trip to Texas to get Kaleb's arm done first, because Dr. Akhom kept insisting that time was running out. The night before we went to Texas, Tom was awakened in the night by a dream. He dreamed that during the nerve surgery something went wrong and Kaleb died. It bothered him so badly that he could not sleep the rest of the night, and could not get the dream out of his head the entire next day.

We took several family members with us on this trip to Texas. Both my parents, Tom's mom, and Mollie went with us to Texas. Everyone was so happy she was going, especially Kaleb.

The airplane ride was wonderful. Everything was going great. We arrived for the third time at Texas Children's Hospital for yet another surgery. Kaleb was taken to be pre-admitted. Dr. Akhom came in to chat with us before taking Kaleb back to surgery. Tom was still concerned about his dream, so he mentioned it to Dr. Akhom. "I hope you don't think I'm crazy, but I just can't live with myself if I don't tell you about the dream I had about this surgery." Dr. Akhom was very humble and said, "I don't think you're crazy at all. I firmly believe that God speaks to us in many different ways. I will have some x-rays taken of Kaleb's neck and have a pediatric orthopedic surgeon look at them before I do anything. I will be moving Kaleb's head around during this surgery, and I don't want to take any chances. Let's just make sure this was just a dream."

So down to the x-ray room we went. This took longer than hoped, so surgery was postponed to the next day. We were all a little disappointed with this, but we have grown to know that all things will work out according to God's timetable and not our own. So we went back to the hotel room to wait until the next morning. Kaleb was scheduled at 9:00 a.m. the next day to have the surgery, depending on what the orthopedic surgeon found out from the x-rays.

Around 9:00 p.m. that night we received a call from Dr. Wilson, a resident working with Dr. Akhom, telling us to come in at 5:00 a.m. instead of 9:00 a.m. We were not sure what was going on. We arrived on time to find that the orthopedic surgeon had ordered a CAT scan and MRI to get a better look. After these tests were run, we were sent back to the waiting room to await test results.

Soon a new doctor walked into the room and asked if Kaleb Davis was there. Kaleb stood up and said, "Yes, I'm Kaleb." The doctor was standing about eight feet from us and asked Kaleb if he could take any steps on his own. Kaleb stood up and walked over to him, and the doctor asked us to come back with him. Tom, Kaleb, and I all walked back, and, by this time, the doctor was almost in tears. He took a long breath and said, "They told me downstairs that this child was walking and to be honest with you, I laughed. I said that there was no way he is walking. I have studied the tests that have been run, and I am here to tell you that God Almighty Himself has laid a hand on this child. There is NOTHING in his spinal cord that is allowing him to walk. I simply would not believe it if I had not seen it myself. However, because of this, I have advised Dr. Akhom that doing this surgery would indeed paralyze Kaleb and would also stand a good chance of killing him." We all just sat there and cried together.

I was crying out of disappointment of course, but also out of relief. God had once again put things in Tom's heart, and placed us in the hands of God-fearing doctors who chose to listen to God rather than their pride.

Kaleb loves football. Before the accident, he played football all year long. It was what he did. He was on a team during the football season, and when the season was over he was always practicing to get ready for the next year. Tom and I knew those days were over, however, we had not had the heart to let Kaleb know yet. The orthopedic doctor had no way of knowing this, so without thinking he said to Kaleb, "You will be fine after getting your neck fused. I mean you'll never play football or anything like that, but you will be able to do a lot of things." Kaleb started to cry. Dr. Akhom spoke very softly to Kaleb and offered him encouragement. The hurt was still there and all we could do was cry.

As Kaleb's tears started to fall, I held him in my arms and told him we would be okay. I looked up and saw Katie standing there. She came over and reminded Kaleb of all the prayers they had shared together. "You know, Kaleb," she explained, "God knows best. This will all pass, and I will see you the next time you come down." So the trip was really for nothing, other than to show us, once again, that God was in our lives and would continue to take care of Kaleb.

A few days after coming home, we went back to Charlotte and met with Dr. James. He ran some x-rays and found that the doctor in Texas was right. Kaleb's neck had shifted forward and pressure was starting to build. The neck fusion would have to be done soon. We were scheduled for surgery in the middle of May. Kaleb could go back to school, but if anything changed at all we were to report to Dr. James immediately.

So we started, once again, to get some normal routine going. Kaleb, thank God, was able to go to school on a regular basis and do some of his school work. He needed a lot of assistance. The school system hired a lady to spend the day with Kaleb and help him with his class time. I had done a lot of praying about whom they would hire. I wanted someone who had a strong faith in God and would stand firm in our belief that everything would work out according to God's glory. They hired just that person, Tammy Woods. Tammy came into our lives and offered support, as well as motivation for Kaleb. She did what had to be done for Kaleb, but also pushed him to do what he could do on his own.

Not only did Tammy help with Kaleb at school, but she was also involved with the youth at her church. She invited Kaleb and Mollie to the different things her church was involved in. This was a blessing. As you can imagine, Kaleb was fearful of getting back into life. He wanted to spend a lot of time at home and still needed the wheelchair most of the time. Tammy helped him to understand he was made special in God's eyes and had a duty to God to be a witness to the youth. Kaleb still feels very strong about this and has great dreams of leading others to Christ.

Chapter 9

Another Valley, Another Victory

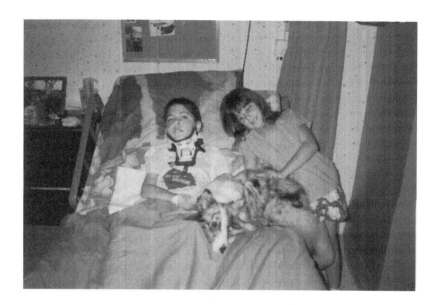

Kaleb was back in school full-time and doing quite well. But on the morning of May 3, 2004, I got the call at work that I had been fearing. I picked up the phone and heard Kaleb's voice on the other end. All he had to say was, "Mom?" and I knew right then something was wrong. He was almost crying when he told me his legs had started to tingle, and he was feeling a little strange. I tried not to panic, because the tingling in his legs was expected. They had tingled before, so we knew that although, this was not a good sign, it was normal for his condition.

"Okay, Kaleb, I will call Dr. James and let him know. Do you think you'll be okay to stay at school?" I knew if I let him hear fear in my voice it would all be over, and we would all fall apart. He said he didn't know for sure, but this time it did feel different from the times before. I decided to call the doctor, balance my cash drawer at the bank, and go get Kaleb. I didn't get Dr. James, but left a message, and went on with balancing out my money so I could pick up my frightened little boy. Before

I finished Tammy called and said, "Laneice, I think you should come on and get Kaleb. He needs you. He needs you right now!" I could hear the panic in her voice and almost dropped to my knees right there. I just grabbed my pocket book and started to cry as I turned to Dana, my supervisor, and said, "I gotta go. Kaleb is in trouble. I gotta go now!!"

Dana was helping a very sweet customer with a transaction at the time. They both looked at me and Dana said, "Okay, just go on. I'll take care of everything here." Then with tears in her eyes, the customer humbly turned to me and said, "I'll be praying for you and your family." I felt God's love in this dear lady's eyes; and I knew beyond a shadow of doubt that this dear Christian would do just that—pray for my family. Once again, I felt the peace that passeth all understanding.

With emergency flashers blinking wildly and my speed increasing, I was off to Blue Ridge Elementary. I did nothing but drive and pray. It was all I could do. I pulled up to the school to find Kaleb and Tammy sitting outside. I am not sure which one looked the most scared. So with a deep breath and power from God, I walked up to them and said, "So, you want to lay out of school do ya? Well, this is one sure way of doing it." My comments seemed to break the ice a little, but Kaleb rolled those big brown, helpless eyes up to me and said, "Mommy, am I going to be okay?" "Yes, Kaleb of course you are. You're fine. We will go down and let Dr. James take a look, and he will know just what to do. You are going to be fine."

You, as a reader, may be asking yourself how I could make that statement to Kaleb. You may wonder how I could make a promise without really knowing all the medical facts yet. I'll tell you how. On the way to Blue Ridge School, I rolled my big blue, helpless eyes up to God and said, "God, is he going to be okay?" And God said, "Yes, of course he is."

Now with Kaleb in the back seat of my car and a folded wheelchair in the trunk, we were off to pick Tom up at work and head straight to Charlotte. I left instructions at work for my cell phone number to be given to the doctor, when he returned my call. I called our parents and made arrangements for Mollie to be picked up after school. Poor little Mollie, once again someone other than Mom and Dad would be taking care of her. Would she complain? No, I knew she would be fine. She has more faith than any little girl I have ever met and a great love for her brother.

We arrived at Dr. James' office and had the usual x-rays and tests run. What we feared most was coming true. Kaleb's neck had slipped even further forward, causing more pressure on the spinal cord. Surgery was needed sooner than we thought. So, Kaleb was admitted to the hospital with surgery scheduled for the next day, May 5, 2004.

I prayed that God would take control of Dr. James' hands and perform the surgery through them. There was no medical guarantee that the surgery would work and life-threatening risks were involved. I remember praying, "God, please just show Dr. James Your power. Let him feel You working through him, and please just do this surgery for him. Please let it go better than even he can imagine. I trust You to do this."

A lot of family came down and spent the morning with us. We all sat in the waiting room and did what we had grown pretty good at doing—waiting and praying. Finally after about three hours into the surgery, the phone rang and it was Dr. James. He had completed the first part of the surgery and so far everything looked good. "Just keep waiting and praying. I'll let you know when we are finished," he said. So that's just what we did.

After about six hours, Dr. James came to get us. We walked with him toward a small room and I thought to myself, *Oh, no, not that little room. God, please don't make us go into that room.* As if he read my mind, Dr. James turned and said, "Kaleb is doing great. The surgery, I think, was a success. Let's just go in here out of the way, so I can show you the x-rays." God is always bailing me out when I am the weakest. He always seems to know just when to send the words I need to hear.

Dr. James said, "If I had sat down yesterday and wrote out exactly how I wanted this surgery to go, I would not have even dreamed of it going as well as it did. It was like everything just fell into place and like someone was just guiding every single thing in that room." I quietly said, "Thanks again, God. I sure do love You."

We were sent upstairs and things were looking pretty good. Kaleb's voice sounded funny. They had moved around his vocal cords during surgery, and he sounded like a robot. This would eventually get better, but it was strange to hear him talking like this. He slept a lot during the night and was doing good the next morning. But as the day progressed, he kept acting more and more strange.

All Kaleb did was sleep. When he woke up, he could not really have a conversation with us. We tried to talk to him, but he would just look at us. At first, I thought he was just playing around, but as time went on, I realized something was definitely not right. We had the floor resident paged, and he said that Kaleb was just still sleepy from the surgery. However, even the nurse agreed with us that it could be more than that. Fortunately, Dr. James' office is attached to the hospital, so Tom walked over and caught him between patients. He said, "As soon as I see my last patient I will come over and check on Kaleb."

By the time he got there, there was no question; something bad was wrong. Kaleb was talking out of his head. He did not know his name; he did not know us; he didn't know anything at all. Dr. James ordered a CAT-scan immediately. He said, "I didn't want to tell you this, because I know how nervous you were with surgery, but we had to put him in something like the halo to do the surgery. I am afraid one of the pins may have punctured another blood vessel like in Winston. I'll let you know something as soon as I can."

Dr. James turned to go downstairs to the CAT-scan room to set things up for us. The nurses were busy unhooking machines and monitors to wheel Kaleb downstairs. My mom was on one side of his bed, and the rest of us were out in the hall waiting for Kaleb. I heard the nurse unplug the machine that monitored Kaleb's vital signs, and it always made a loud alarm when this was done. I knew the alarm would scare Kaleb, so I ran back into the room to let him know that everything was okay. He let out a loud whimper; the sound is tuck in my mind to this day. What happened next was one of the scariest things I have ever witnessed in my life. Kaleb's entire face drew to the left and he was unrecognizable. He began to convulse violently. I started screaming, "Something's wrong, something's wrong. Get help now!"

The nurse ran to the door and yelled for help. Nurses from everywhere came running. We were in the doorway of the room while this was taking place, so they just pushed his bed back inside and began working with him. I stood helpless. One of the nurses turned to the other and said, "Call a code blue for me." I remember grabbing her arm and saying, "Don't you dare call a code blue on him. Don't you dare call that!" I was so terrified. I did not want to hear that. Then reality took hold, and I knew it had to be done. I turned loose of the nurse's arm, and she ran to the intercom. "Code blue, North tower room 27. Code blue, North tower room 27. Code blue, North tower room 27." This was repeated three times and by now I was in the middle of the hall screaming, "God, please, no. Not now. We've come so far. God, please not now."

God already knew what was going to happen, so He had placed a doctor on the floor that specialized in children's respiratory. This doctor and several others were in the room working on Kaleb, before the nurse even got out the third 'code blue.' I have never seen anything like it. These professionals had no doubt practiced this drill, because all the equipment was brought in and placed at certain locations, and everyone knew exactly what their job was and they were doing it.

Tom was running down the hall yelling for Dr. James, who by this time was sprinting back to Kaleb's room. They sent us all into an empty room next to Kaleb's. Oh, what crying and praying we were doing. The chaplain and social worker were in the room with us. Mollie sat shaking on my lap, and I just held her close and said, "Kaleb is going to be okay. He will be fine." Mollie rolled her big brown eyes up at me, much the same way her brother had, and said, "Mommy, is Kaleb going to die?" I looked down at her and gathered all the strength I could, and said, "No, Mollie, Kaleb is not going to die. He just needs some extra help right now. God has sent his helpers in to do their job. Kaleb will be better in no time at all. You'll see. Everyone will see. It won't be long."

I had to sign some papers allowing them to place a trach in Kaleb's neck, because they could not insert the breathing tube down his throat. The surgery had left the inside of his neck very swollen. The trach was inserted so they could take him down to the operating room and do brain surgery. I remember as I signed the form for Dr. James, looking up at him and saying, "This is not his brain, doctor. I know it is not his brain. I have seen him with a brain injury and I know this is not his brain." He looked and me and said, "I pray to God you're right."

We were sent downstairs to wait in the consultation room—the room I hate. The chaplain came with us, and we all just sat and prayed. We waited for what seemed like hours, but was only about 30 minutes when the door opened and in walked Dr. James. He was smiling. He said, "Well, Mom, you were right. It's not his brain. His sodium has dropped. When someone's sodium drops to around 17, they will have convulsions. Kaleb's is at 14. This is a deadly number, but we have caught it in time, and hopefully, there will be no side effects from this. He is going up to the PICU to get an IV that will build his sodium back up. However, we must do it slowly. He will be in there a day or two. I know you've been through a lot today. Try to get some rest. If you don't mind, I am going home now to spend some time with my son. I really just want to go home and hold him. I'll be back in the morning." I walked over to him and gave him a big hug and said, "You go home and tell your son I said that his daddy is a great doctor, and Kaleb Davis thinks so too." At that, he began crying as he walked down the hall to go home.

So on May 6, 2004, we found ourselves once again sleeping in the floor of a PICU waiting room. I fell asleep that night praising God for coming to the rescue yet another time.

Days turned to weeks, and Kaleb remained in the hospital from May 5, through May 30, 2004. We went home exactly one year to the day of the accident itself. The trach was gone, and all that was left was a pretty bad scar and another victory for the Lord.

We scheduled the next nerve graph surgery in Texas for July 13, 2004. This time my mom, Tom's mom, and Mollie went down with us. Again, everything went smoothly. Dr. Akhom did the surgery. He took a nerve from Kaleb's left leg, and attached one end to the nerve that feeds his left lung, and the other end to the nerve that would feed his triceps, and everything below his elbow. The surgery went well. The only thing that alarmed the doctor was the possibility that he might have scraped Kaleb's lung during the surgery. So for precaution, he inserted a chest tube and put Kaleb in the PICU unit in Texas. Time proved this to be just a precaution, and the tube was removed. We were sent home, and time would tell what the results of this surgery would be.

Chapter 10

Our God is Awesome

Time has passed now. Kaleb no longer needs a wheelchair, but he does have a difficult time. I do not like to talk about the negative, and I do hate to sound like I'm complaining. We have been so blessed. However, it is not the perfect picture that I had in my mind. I think every parent imagines their child just doing normal things. We, as an entire family, have had to realize that is not what God has planned for us. Kaleb has many complications. Most of these complications come from his brain injury. It destroyed most of his muscles. When he woke up from the coma, all he really had the strength to move were his eyelids for a week or so. He could whisper a few words and that was about it.

Now, because of the weakened muscles, his hamstring stays very tight. So tight, in fact, that we have to stretch it every night. Unfortunately, I am not strong enough to do this, so Tom has to take the responsibility. Kaleb lays on his back, and Tom has to raise Kaleb's leg up with his foot pointing toward the ceiling. His leg will only go up to about a 45 degree angle. Once it is at this position, the leg has to be pushed as hard as possible, and held for about two or three minutes. This is difficult to do without injuring him further. Tom has to be careful not to pull Kaleb's muscle. He has had several injections of Botox in his leg. This, however, does little to help. He has a foot brace that he wears during the day, that keeps his toes from dropping as he walks and also give just a little stretch to the hamstring. He also has two leg braces he wears at night to keep his legs as straight as possible. In addition to these two leg braces at night, he also has a foot brace he wears to lock his foot in a 90 degree angle while he sleeps. Because, he cannot turn his head at all due to the neck fusion, he has to try and sleep on his side or back. So you can imagine having to sleep either on your side or back all night long, with both legs kept straight and your foot at 90 degrees. His covers get tangled up in the braces, and he cannot move very well.

Then there are the bowel and bladder problems. It is impossible for him to get up and walk with these braces on, so we have made some accommodations to help with this. But what an amazing attitude he has. He never complains; he just takes it in stride, and calls out to me during the night if he needs help.

Kaleb longs to look and feel normal. I think this has been the hardest for him. He has a severe limp, and his spine is curved more than 80 degrees. So it is hard to get clothes to fit him the way they should. He also has a brace he has to wear around his chest with a piece that holds his left arm in place. It is hard to get shirts, pants, and shoes that will fit him.

Kaleb still cannot use his left arm, but doctors are hopeful that in time he will be able to gain some function again. He is able to feel his left shoulder and can shrug. For the most part this is completely healed. He has sensation in his upper arm. If a pillow is placed between his ribs and upper left arm he is able to hold onto it using his biceps and triceps. A muscle transplant is the next step the doctors want to take. Kaleb is still not strong enough for this surgery. He needs to gain more weight before the transplant can be done. Below his elbow and into his hand he has slight sensatation, but cannot tell what part of this area has been touched. There is some movement in his wrist, however it is very slight and will probably need muscle transplants as well.

But enough of the complaining . . .

Long hours of therapy, loving therapists, and support of family and friends have brought us to the point we are at today. Kaleb has made great strides, with the help of God. He is 17 years old now, and has his driver's license. He is able to do a lot of things that we were told would never happen. Kaleb is an outdoors man. Next to playing sports, his passion has always been hunting and fishing. With help from friends, family, and special equipment, Kaleb is able to hunt and fish. All of our friends and neighbors have given him unlimited hunting rights on their property. This is an amazing offer considering most of these men are avid hunters themselves.

More importantly, God Himself has been with us from the beginning and will remain with us until the end.

I would like to ask you to read the first part of this book one more time. Remember the Bible verse I had written in my journal; the one about the BRANCH? Isn't it funny how the tree limb caused the most agonizing three years of my life, but Jesus, or the "BRANCH" gave me the most peace I have ever felt.

Many Thanks

Thank you does not seem like enough to say. I only pray that each person who helped us through this valley will be blessed with the mountain top we are on now. I dare not try to mention all by name, but know that everything that was done (a lot that we probably don't even know about) is very much appreciated.

To the doctors and nurses: Thank you for letting the Lord lead you and for not giving up. Your professionalism is only exceeded by your faith in God. Thank you for loving my child.

To First Citizens Bank and Randy G. Rhodes & Associates: Thank you for understanding that Tom and I needed to be with our son rather than be at work. Your patience with us is greatly appreciated. Hopefully, we can repay you by being dedicated employees who will fulfill our employment obligations with Christian principles.

To Preacher Ted Reynolds and dear Sister Ann: Thank you, thank you, thank you. You have become a part our family. The strength that you brought down the mountain with every visit will never be forgotten.

To Danny, Dreama, Daniel, Summer, Dustin, Carrie, and Dylan Farmer: Thanks guys for being the friends we needed. In good times and bad, you stuck with us. Now, let's go camping again!!!!

To Mark, Julie, Nathan, and Levi Shepherd: Your support of us is matchless. I don't know how we would have made it through without your visits and encouragement. By the way, sorry, Mark, about feeding that annoying cat; but he really did appreciate all you did for him.

To Ashe County Schools, Tammy Woods, Jeanne Caviness, and the entire Exceptional Children Department: How could we have gotten where we are without you? All of you have gone beyond the call of duty to help Kaleb. You have all taught him far more than what can be learned in a book.

To Kalen Fulbright, Diane Gollot, Emily Morley, and Martin Little: Kaleb would not be where he is today without therapist and trainers like you. You have impacted Kaleb's life with your patience and motivation. Keep up the good work! You have not even once let him down.

To Mark Shepherd's Masonry and Timber Solutions: How much we do appreciate the sidewalk and ramp. It served as a great help with the wheelchair and is still helping Kaleb today.

To Yvette Jones: Kaleb's hair would have been down to his waist if you had not come and trimmed it. Thank you for not only cutting his hair, but loving him also.

To everyone who had a part in the auctions: Thank you from the bottom of our hearts. We are still using the money to go to Texas and pay for medical expenses. May God bless you all for your selfless giving.

To Sturgill's Baptist Church: Thank you for being our 'church family' and guiding us in the Lord so we would have the strength to get through this.

To Tuckerdale Baptist Church: Your leadership in our life now is what keeps us going. You have taught us many things, but most importantly the love of one another.

To Ashe County: Wow, we found friends we never even knew we had. Your prayers and concern was overwhelming; not only to us, but to the many people we met in Winston, Charlotte, and Texas. No one could believe that such a place even existed. The unity you showed touched more lives than you will ever know. (Look for a population growth—everyone asked where Ashe County was!!)

To Sandy Pinto, and Julian, Sara, Corrie, and Joshua Owen: Thanks so much for all the help with editing. I know it was not an easy job, but you made it seem easy. I love you guys!

To Nathan and Levi Shepherd, Dustin Roten, Daniel Farmer, and the entire student body in Ashe County Schools: Thanks for all your support. Thanks to you, Kaleb never had to worry about coming back to school. He was always met with open arms and supportive friends. Most people your age would not understand how difficult things had become for Kaleb. You took him in as if he had not been injured. That means the world to our family, and especially Kaleb.

To our Family: Parents, grandparents, aunts, uncles, and cousins: There is really no way of ever thanking the ones you love the most for doing what comes natural. We could not make it through this without you. Your help is much more than appreciated. We love you all.

Most important: Thanks be to GOD. Without You nothing would even matter. Thank You for creating us, and not just stopping with that. You are forever watching over us, and protecting us, and I am sorry to say that You do not get as much credit as You deserve. I have learned a great many things about You during this time. Perhaps one of the greatest things is that no matter what we do on this earth, no matter what our education level is, no matter what our banking account holds, or how many friends we THINK we have, we own nothing. You supply all our needs as we need them. Of all the gifts that were given to us by friends and family, all the wonderful gifts the doctors and nurses were blessed with to save Kaleb's life, and, yes, even the miracles you gave us, there is one gift that far surpasses all of the above. "For God so loved the world that He gave His only begotten Son that whosoever believeth on Him should not perish, but have everlasting life." (John 3:16). All praise and honor goes to our Heavenly Father who loved us this much.

EPILOGUE

The last six years of my life have been the most difficult years I have had thus far. It has been filled with a lot of different emotions, and they have each taken a toll on me and my family. We began the year in 2003, taking a lot of things for granted. It all changed with one single windstorm. Since that time, it has been one 'windstorm' after another. There are really no words that could possibly tell the complete story of what we have gone through. I have tried to express as much of these emotions as I can but still feel I have come short. My desire in writing this is to give hope to those of you who may be going through a valley right now. We don't always get the life we've dreamed about, and circumstances can certainly change in the blink of an eye.

Our circumstances changed several times throughout this valley that we have faced. One such circumstance was finding out in 2005, that a lot of Kaleb's injuries were the direct results of mistakes that were made at the hospital. These mistakes, although not intentional, left us with a lot of questions about Kaleb's future.

It became difficult to give him the care that he needed, simply, because we could not afford the equipment, therapy, and time that it took to give Kaleb every opportunity to defeat his physical handicaps. With this heavy burden on our hearts, we once again turned to the Lord. We asked His guidance. After this we talked with our pastor and several Christian friends, and we made the very difficult decision to pursue legal action against Wake Forest University Hospital.

We have a very close friend who is an attorney, David Jolly. Tom spoke with David about our situation, and David suggested we meet with Clifford Britt. Cliff is an attorney in Winston-Salem, who is very familiar with medical malpractice. He decided to take a look into Kaleb's case. With a lot of research, Cliff was able to uncover things that had happened during Kaleb's stay at the hospital that Tom and I had no idea had taken place. Yes, we knew when we left the hospital that there were mistakes; some were obvious, and others were hinted at by friends we made who worked for the hospital. However, a review of the medical records, revealed that most of Kaleb's injuries, except for the left arm, were a result of bad judgements and careless decisions. It took three years of work by Cliff, and the staff at Comerford and Britt Law firm to uncover what had been done.

Another attorney who was instrumental in our case was John Chilson, who also works for Comerford and Britt. John and Cliff spent a lot time working for us. Not only were they our legal council, but they became so much more. We grew very fond of them and built a strong friendship. This was a very difficult time in our lives, because we are not the type of people who are out for a lawsuit in hopes of getting rich. We simply needed help in providing Kaleb with the things his care required.

John and Cliff both helped so much with this. Not only did they get a verdict in our favor, but they opened many other doors for us. Through the expert witnesses they hired, we learned that there are many more options out there for Kaleb. We met many experts in the medical profession and gained a deeper knowledge about Kaleb's injuries. Not only did they show us why Kaleb had some of the obstacles he faces, but they also gave options to overcome these difficulties. David, John, Cliff, and the entire staff at Comerford and Britt were there for us every step of the way. They were our support through one of the most difficult decisions we have ever had to make.

All of a sudden, we were staring right into the eyes of truth. We had to take a hard look at what was going on with Kaleb and be truthful about the difficulties we face on a day-to-day basis with him. It was something I, for one, was not good at doing. As you probably can already tell, I am the type of person who looks for the positive and tries to ignore the negative. This is not meant to be a compliment to myself, on the contrary, it is a weakness. I do not like to face the reality of Kaleb's handicaps. But with these new found friends and their support, we made it through.

I have spent a lot of time deciding whether or not to include this part of our lives in this manuscript. On one hand, I thought it best to leave out, because I do not want to give the impression that the hospital is not an outstanding hospital; it is. There are many professionals there and the wealth of knowledge in that place is amazing. However, on the other hand most of you reading this already know of the lawsuit and the outcome due to media. It would seem hypocritical of me to just leave it out. Besides, it is a part of our story. It shows how you have to do some things in life that may go against every part of you, but it must be done to help out someone you love.

Kaleb before the accident

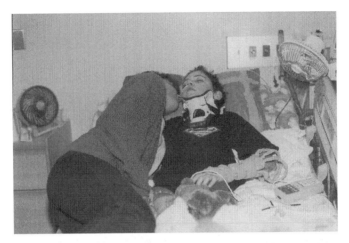
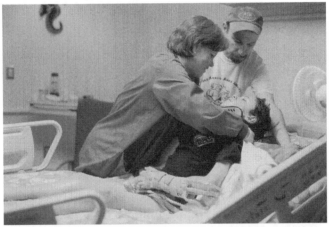
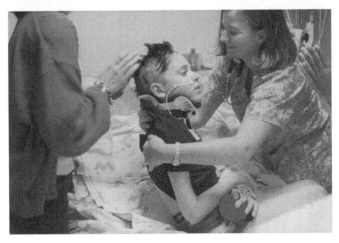

Kaleb in Winston Salem

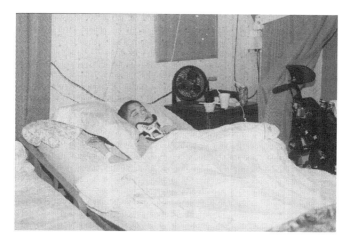
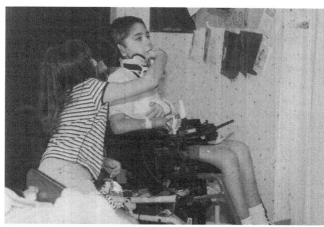
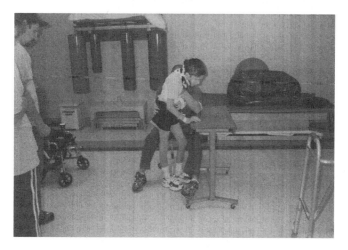

Kaleb in Charlotte

Kaleb coming home

Kaleb today

Made in the USA
Lexington, KY
12 January 2014